Guided by Grief

From Parental Loss to Professional Purpose

HEATHER HIGGINS

BlueRose ONE.com
Stories Matter

BLUEROSE PUBLISHERS UK Ltd.
London

This book is primarily published and distributed in Great Britain and is also available in other global marketplaces.

BlueRose ONE.com
Stories Matter

ISBN: 978-93-7542-060-6

Designed and distributed by **BlueRoseONE.com** with global reach. Printing and fulfilment are managed through international distribution networks, ensuring availability based on order locations.

For publishing inquiries, visit www.BlueRoseONE.com

BlueRose Publishers UK Ltd,
Unit 3, 6-7 St Mary at Hill, London

+44 7386286323

First Edition: April 2026

This book is dedicated to anyone who has experienced or is currently experiencing loss, grief, or bereavement.

Especially my two incredible, brave and resilient siblings – Louise and Christopher. You will never know how proud I am of you both. I love you both with all my heart and more.

Us against the world x

Introduction:

Grief has a way of arriving uninvited. It doesn't knock politely or ask if it's an appropriate time for you. It turns your world upside down, suddenly, completely, and without warning. It stops time and leaves you questioning everything you thought you knew. Nothing prepares you for it. Nothing. Grief touches people of every age, background, belief, location, occupation and circumstance. Grief does not discriminate. When it hits, it can feel like you are the only person in the world going through it, and that can be a very dark and lonely place.

I know that feeling well.

I've been there. In the silence, in the confusion, in the weight of it all. I've felt the kind of ache that doesn't go away with time, only changes shape. I've cried alone in the car, smiled through the pain at family gatherings or friends' parties, and lay awake at night replaying memories that suddenly felt like lifelines I was desperately holding onto.

My relationship with grief began as a child and has followed me into adulthood, shaping who I am in ways both devastating and unexpectedly transformative.

This book, *Guided by Grief*, weaves together two parts of me: the person who has lived through multiple personal losses, and the professional who has had the privilege of walking alongside others in their grief, as a counsellor and a life coach.

This is not a manual. You won't find 'five simple steps to healing' or instructions for 'getting over it.' Grief doesn't work that way. However, there have been times when I wished there was such a simple solution. Instead, these pages hold a collection of stories, reflections, and truths. Some raw, some tender, all real – shared with the intention to provide a gentle companionship for anyone navigating the messy, difficult and unpredictable path of grief.

Within these pages are moments of intense vulnerability, pain and breakthrough. I share what helped me and what didn't. What surprised me and what I am still trying to understand. Because grief isn't linear. It is messy, and it is erratic. It ebbs and flows. Some days, you feel like you're making tremendous progress; other days might feel like you are trying to survive. And sometimes, it feels like you're right back at the beginning. All of it is completely normal. We are only human.

You may be reading this book because you have lost someone or something you care about. Maybe you are in the thick of it, trying to navigate a new bereavement, or maybe you are ready to start your healing journey from a past bereavement that perhaps hasn't been fully processed.

Or maybe someone you love is grieving, and you're trying to understand what they are going through to offer your support to them during this difficult period. Whatever brought you here, I want you to know this: you don't have to carry this on your own. It's ok to feel sad - there is no possible "right" way to grieve. And while every person's experience of grief is unique, there are threads of understanding and connection that unite us.

Although it is the first thing we often think of, grief is not always the passing of someone we love. You might be grieving for a life you used to live, the way you used to be. You might be grieving the end of a relationship or friendship, or grieving the loss of a job. You might be grieving that you are no longer able to do something you love or grieving a past version of yourself that you miss. Grief comes in many shapes and sizes, and all are valid.

Writing this book for me started as a journalling exercise, yet as I moved through the chapters of my life and my experiences with grief, I was able to tie in my own personal experiences with those of my clients and how I have supported them, combining the two unique perspectives which ultimately created this book - from the reflective and emotional viewpoint of a griever to the professional perspective of a counsellor.

I have had to revisit memories and past experiences that were hidden away and unprocessed for 25 years, which has been a humbling yet healing experience. Bringing back memories I didn't realise were sitting there, still waiting to be understood.

I began writing this book just eight months after the sudden and unexpected loss of a parent. So, the stories within these pages are not reflections from a distant, healed place; they are current, immediate, tender, and still tangled in the rawness of grief - still shifting and still finding its way.

Thank you for picking up this book. Thank you for being willing to sit with difficult emotions. Both mine and yours.

This book is a reminder that even in your darkest moments, healing is possible, not through forgetting or moving past the loss, but through remembering, honouring, and learning to carry your loss with love and compassion, for yourself and others.

So, when your grief feels too heavy to carry, when you feel like you have lost hope, when you feel like the rest of the world has moved on, whenever you feel like you are falling apart or caught up in your own thoughts - I hope that somewhere in these pages you find a glimmer of comfort, connection, and the courage to take the next step, whatever that looks like for you.

Please remember that throughout all of this, you are not alone.

With love
Heather x

Table of Contents

The Day Everything Changed

I was 9 years old when the world started to change around me. Old enough to know something was going on, but not old enough to comprehend. My dad was diagnosed with Non-Hodgkin Lymphoma, a type of Cancer, at the young age of 38. Now, as an adult myself, it's scary to think that's just a few years older than I am now. So young, too young. Too young to leave his wife and three kids under the age of 10.

I was the oldest at 9 years old, then my younger sister, Louise, who was 6 and my little brother Christopher, who was only 4 at the time.

We had a happy childhood up until then. Before loss reshaped us, our world was small in the best of ways. It was made of ordinary moments that now, through nostalgia, seem so special. Small details in memories that will stay with me forever. My dad's black hair, my mum's red hair. Our childhood bedrooms, our big garden that dad worked so hard to make a fun place for us to play in. The smell of coffee in our living room, my mum cooking dinner for us all, and dad eating his dinner at the table after he finished work. He had his own business as a roofer and rough caster. I remember his work van vividly. The white van with the black and red writing, which read "Anderson Roofing".

We had our safe and loving family home. Our house was full - full of days filled with rushed school mornings, dinners around the table, messy bedrooms, sibling arguments, shared laughter, watching TV and bedtime stories. My mum used to groan whenever dad put us to bed, because he'd scoop us up in a "fireman's lift," carrying us over his shoulder while we giggled uncontrollably - completely wide awake and laughing when we should have been going to sleep.

We loved our family. Mum and Dad were our centre. Steady, loving, fun.

We used to go on holiday as a family to visit mum and dad's friends in Jersey, Ireland and Blackpool. Often, my brain takes me back to those times. The safety of that family unit that no longer exists. The memories often feel hazy or distant. And although nostalgic and often emotional, it's still wonderful to hold on to.

Looking back, we didn't know then how precious all of it was. Children rarely do. We only knew that we felt secure and happy. We felt protected with no reason to believe otherwise. The beauty of our childhood wasn't in big gestures or perfectly posed photographs (I only have 2 photos of the 5 of us all together, the only 2 I know of that exist, and they are certainly not posed or perfect, but it means so much to me now to have had that time captured). We had our loving family around us, and we were safe. Everything was great. Everything was normal.

Until it wasn't.

I vaguely remember changes happening around the house. Dad started to do less, work less. He spent a lot of time in bed and had to use a stick when he was walking. I didn't ask questions, but I noticed all the same. Looking back, these changes started to happen quite quickly. Upon reflection, I don't know if that is because it's something our parents hid from us for a while or whether his illness took over rapidly. Unfortunately, these are questions I will never know the answer to now.

Soon after, the hospital appointments started. And then one day, just like that, Dad moved into the hospital. I didn't realise it at the time, but this must have been him starting his cancer treatment.

I remember mum sitting my sister and me down and telling us,

"Dad's got a new hairstyle, he's got a 'David Beckham.'"

David Beckham, the footballer, at the time had recently shaved all his blonde hair off ("the curtains" which were very much the style in the late 90's/early 2000's) and now had a shaved head. This was mum's gentle way of breaking it to us that dad had lost all his hair due to the cancer treatment, and she was preparing us for when we next visited him in the hospital. She was trying to make light of it and tell us in a way that we wouldn't feel scared about the changes or be afraid of how Dad would look different and not like himself.

One day, I remember being taken out of school to go and speak with one of the nurses at the hospital where Dad was staying. As any 9-year-old would, I was happy that I managed to get the afternoon off school, not realising the seriousness of what was going on. The innocence of it all.

Mum told me ahead of time that I'd be having a chat with a nurse, and that I could ask her anything I wanted about Dad's illness. She said the nurse was there to help me understand what was happening and to answer any questions I had. But I didn't know what to ask. I didn't even know what was happening.

The lovely nurse took me into a small room, away from where Dad lay in his hospital bed with Mum beside him. It was just the nurse and me in that room. She began to explain to me that Dad had a disease, and they were doing everything they could to try to make him better.

When she asked if I had any questions, I could only think of one:

"Why is this happening to him?" I asked.

I feel that this question may have taken her by surprise, because how on earth do you answer that? She paused before replying,

"We don't know. But we're going to do everything we can to try and help him get better."

It's scary for a child knowing their parents are going to the hospital. I see it daily now, working with kids myself as a Children's and Young Persons Counsellor. It is a confusing time as they know something is wrong. Children can often sense it and feel it, but are unable to name it. They don't want to ask their parents about what is happening for fear of upsetting them, and sometimes, they just don't want to know the answers. I can completely empathise with that.

I recently came across a card that I had made for my dad around this time. It was a home-made 'Get Well Soon' card. A yellow piece of thick paper folded over to make the shape of a card. I had drawn pictures on it, and I got my whole primary school class to sign their names to say we were all thinking about him and wishing him a speedy recovery. I remember taking it to him in the hospital. A memory I had completely forgotten about until I saw this yellow piece of card again. Then it all came rushing back to me.

The hospital room, the smell, the colours, the other patients, Dad in his hospital bed.

All repressed childhood memories.

My gran had kept this card all those years. Safely tucked away in her cupboard, where she kept everything else I had ever drawn or written in my life! And I'm so glad she did. When I first saw it and read the words, I started to cry. The emotion hit me like a ton of bricks from nowhere.

'Get Well Soon, Dad'

That innocent little girl had no idea what was to come. She was making her dad a card to let him know that she missed him, and she hoped that he would be feeling better soon and was waiting for him to come back home, where he belonged.

Little did she know, he wasn't coming back home.

After a while, we were told that Dad was moving to St Vincent's Hospice near where we lived. At the time, I didn't know what a hospice was. I thought it was just another word for a hospital. Looking back now, I realise the adults around me were already preparing for a goodbye.

Visiting here had a different feel to it. It was smaller and more intimate than a hospital. Less clinical, more homely. It felt scary, but I couldn't explain why. It just felt different.

The nurses were lovely, and lots of family would visit with us. Maybe that was what made me feel scared at the time.

Why the influx of visitors?

Why the move at all?

Why is Dad getting thinner? He looks so different.

There were so many unanswered questions in that little girl's mind. I dreaded our visits to the hospice. I didn't like the smell. I still remember it to this day. I remember whenever mum would visit on her own, I could smell the place on her jacket when she got home. That smell made me feel sick. It wasn't a terribly bad smell, but it smelled like the hospice, and that was enough to evoke a physical reaction in my body.

The anxiety.

I remember telling my mum I didn't like going. But we still went. In my mum's position, I don't know what I would have done. She was probably torn between knowing we didn't have long left with our dad and the fact that I felt uncomfortable visiting. But we visited.

My memories from this time are hazy, but I remember vividly that I hated even driving past the hospice still for years afterwards. There were too many painful emotions. And even years later, as a teenager, I could feel the physical sensations in my body taking over, taking me back to that time in my childhood. The time when he was in there.

It's all coming back to me even as I write this chapter. The nausea, the nervousness, the unknown.

Then came the lead-up to Christmas. It was the year 2000.

Mum said we'd be going to visit Dad in the hospice on Christmas Day.

I was devastated. Leaving the house on Christmas was unheard of for us. We had always stayed at home. Gran and Pap (mum's parents), Uncle Barry (mum's brother), Auntie Lisa (his wife), Gran Anderson (dad's mum) and Auntie Mary (my gran's sister) would all come over and spend the day at our house with us. Every year, every celebration. Every birthday, every Christmas. Those memories were so incredibly happy. I still look back on those times with so much love, especially when I come across old photographs. Reminding me of those happy times in our lives. We were truly blessed with an amazing family.

So, I was upset about going to the hospice on Christmas Day. But looking back, I see that my feelings weren't just about breaking tradition. The emotions ran much deeper. It was the changes that were happening. I wanted something constant, something I knew would be the same, something I could rely on. In the middle of all the chaos and uncertainty that was happening around us. Surely Christmas Day, the day I look forward to all year, as most kids do, would be a day of regularity.

I recently found another card I had made for my Dad. A Christmas card this time. Another card I am glad my gran kept all this time, for me to now be able to reminisce, reflect and process what was going on for me at that time. Cards, I had no recollection of writing, but as they appear in front of me now, I begin to remember.

The card reads:

"To Dad,

I hope you get better soon. I hope you like the Christmas card. Our Christmas won't be good without you. And I hope you like the Christmas presents I will get you. I will not tell you what it is.

Lots of lots of lots of love and kisses

Heather"

The childish wording and way of writing make me emotional. As I write this, I just want to go back in time and hug that little girl. The innocence, the naivety, with no idea of what was coming or how her life was about to change forever.

I didn't realise it at the time, but that Christmas Day would be the last time I ever saw my dad.

I've tried to block this memory out of my head because it didn't look like him. But that memory will always be there. How thin he was, how strange he looked to me. In all honesty, I was scared. That's why I didn't want to see him or visit the hospice. The changes scared me.

This comes with an immense amount of guilt that I have been carrying for a long time. I can only imagine that Dad was desperate to see his kids as often as possible during this time, yet I didn't want to be there.

I often need to remind myself that I was a child and I was dealing with things the only way I could at the time.

My 9-year-old brain couldn't cope with what was happening. I couldn't process it.

Reflecting now, I wish I could go back to that time. I would spend the whole day with him, every day and never, ever want to leave.

After that Christmas, for the first week in January, my sister and I stayed with our family friends, our best friends, the McPhees.

We met them due to Kirsty and me being in the same dance class when we were toddlers. We became best friends and still are to this day. Our mums immediately became friends, were pregnant with our younger sisters at the same time, and when the girls were born, they became best friends too and still are. Our dads were also good friends and used to go to the pub together, and would often take us all out on walks together. We have some great childhood memories of this time.

They weren't just friends; they were like extended family.

That week in January 2001, we thought it was great getting to stay with them for days, as normally it was only a one-night sleepover, and then home time. Although we usually tried every trick in the book to stay at each other's houses for longer than the intended visit. I remember once we were all down at their house, the 5 of us, and when it was time for us to leave and walk home to our own house, we tried to hide all of our families' shoes in a cupboard so we couldn't leave! Great times and memories were had. But this wasn't a normal time.

Around 4th Jan, I remember their dad saying -

"I'm going to take you both up to see your Mum, then I'll bring you back here if you want".

Even as I'm writing this, I can feel the physiological changes in my body. The anxiety. The racing heart. The churning of my stomach. Taking me back to that day.

The Day Everything Changed.

When we arrived back at our home, I immediately knew something was wrong. All of my dad's brothers and sisters were there. He came from a big family. He was the youngest of 7 children. Mum took Louise and me into the kitchen and broke the news that our dad had passed away. I still remember so very clearly my exact reply.

"Can we still go and stay at Kirsty's house?"

That's it. That was my answer to that.

I wanted to escape. To run away from it. I wanted to get out of that house, away from the upset visitors. Away from everyone and their sympathetic looks and the look of their own grief, tears and sadness. It was all too much. I just wanted out. I just wanted my best friend. I wanted things to go back to how they were an hour ago. But things were not going to go back to how they were. Not ever again.

I don't have many other memories of that day, but I remember that night very well. We were all in the bedroom ready to sleep, Kirsty and I, her sister Eilidh and my sister Louise, and I remember my 6-year-old sister asking the question -

"Will my dad get his hair back in Heaven?"

And I just broke down. Sobbing uncontrollably. I cried for the first time since hearing the devastating news earlier that day.

What a horribly innocent question for a 6-year-old to wonder. It still makes me sad to this day when I think of her asking that.

Lorna and Stewart took me downstairs and sat with me, talking with me and let me cry. I will always be grateful to them for their support and kindness. I'll never forget that night, and they must have been a huge help to my mum during this time.

The next day was when it really hit me. When we went back home to our own house. That realisation that it's just the 4 of us now. Any hopes or wishes of Dad ever coming back home and things being back to normal were gone forever.

Everything really has changed.

Childhood Grieving

While dad was in the hospice, I remember a woman taking Louise and me into a quiet room. She handed us booklets to be filled out, blank notepads and pens and told us we could draw or write anything we wanted. We were nine and six. My recollections of this time are still hazy, but as I move through these chapters, the memories that have been buried away for all these years reappear, and suddenly it feels like I'm right back there, in that room in the hospice.

I didn't realise it then, but this was a children's counselling service.

Years later, in my late teens, my gran told me that during one of those sessions, I had drawn a tiny house. I kind of remember it. A tiny house, with tiny windows, a tiny door and a tiny garden with a path leading up to the front door. As if it were far away in the distance. The adults were told that it represented how far away I felt from everything. How I was pushing away what was happening around me, and perhaps didn't want to acknowledge the changes.

That revelation struck something in me. 10 years later, it was like a lightbulb moment. That *is* what I was doing. I didn't want to face what was going on at the time. What nine-year-old would? I wanted to detach myself from it.

It astonished me that something as simple as a drawing could express such deep emotion from a child's perspective. That moment planted a seed: **this is what I want to do with my life.** Help others. People who are grieving, suffering, and navigating change. People who are going through what I have been through.

I recently came across those notepads and booklets; the ones the counsellor had given to my sister and me. My mum had kept them all these years. I opened them without knowing what I would see, but after I did, suddenly those memories came rushing back to me. It was a profound moment looking through those pages as an adult. What we had written when we were children, and in the midst of the confusion and sadness about dad being ill and being in the hospice. It felt like looking through a window into a younger version of myself. A child, trying to make sense of what was happening around her. In some ways, it was heartbreaking. It still makes me feel emotional to think of those booklets and those two little girls who wrote in them.

On the pages, we listed what made us happy, what made us sad, what frightened us and what we wished for. There were drawings of my dad in his bed in the hospice and sentences that tailed off unfinished as if we couldn't quite find the language for what we were feeling. At that age, words such as 'anticipatory grief' or 'bereavement' didn't exist for us. But we had those booklets – our first attempt at expressing the inexpressible.

As I read, I realised that these pages were my first experience of counselling. Not as a practitioner, but as someone in need. Even then, writing offered a kind of quiet relief. The act of putting thoughts on paper was easier than saying them out loud. I've always been a very private person, and I've always enjoyed writing, so I will always advocate for journaling through emotions because it is such a great tool to help us make sense of our thoughts and feelings. I didn't know it at the time, but I was already learning that feelings deserved space, that our story mattered.

Finding those booklets felt like discovering a thread which has been connected to me throughout my life. One that connects me to the little girl I was then and the woman I am now. They revealed the roots of my passion for counselling were planted much earlier than I realised. It is connected to the part of me that sat in that hospice room, trying to understand why the world was changing. Proof to me that my journey into counselling was not accidental.

It began long before the training courses, before the theories, before I had the language for grief. It began with two little girls, pens in hand, trying to hold onto their dad the only way they knew how.

I remember having about a week off school after dad passed away and then returning to 'normal'. Whatever 'normal' meant now.

Looking back on my childhood grieving process, I know I spent a long time pushing everything to the back of my mind. I wanted to pretend things were fine. I was never someone who liked attention. I was a shy and quiet child, especially at school and in front of crowds. My thinking was: if I act like everything's okay, maybe it will be.

After my dad's passing, my mum arranged for a children's counsellor to come to our house to speak to me alone every week.

Before each session, I used to listen to Atomic Kitten's *Whole Again* CD on repeat. It must have been the popular song of the time, and I was thrilled to have bought the 'single' CD. Something nostalgic in itself because CDs are no longer a thing, and sadly, something the next generation will probably never know. That thrill of going to Woolworths and spending your pocket money on the latest singles from the top 10. A regular Saturday trip we would make with my gran and Auntie Mary.

Now, I can't bear to hear that Atomic Kitten song. It instantly transports me back to that time.

Our brains like to form associations so quickly, especially during emotionally intense experiences. When our senses are tied to an event, they can create a trigger response if we experience it again. Something we hear (Atomic Kitten), something we smell (the smell of the hospice or a fragrance someone used to wear), something we see (maybe a photograph or an item that belonged to them) or taste (perhaps a meal you used to enjoy together) can instantly transport us back to that emotional time in our lives, and we suddenly feel the same way we did when the event was actually happening. It often evokes a physiological response (heart rate increasing, feeling nauseous or lightheaded).

That song for me became tied to grief and to the pressure I felt to talk about something I wasn't ready to face.

Looking back as a counsellor now, I know my mum was doing what she thought was best. She wanted me to have support to help me through this period, and she was right to do so. She was probably encouraged to do so by the hospice and school. But

I didn't feel comfortable. I didn't feel safe enough in that space. I didn't want to talk. I wasn't ready to acknowledge what had happened.

That is one of the most valuable lessons I've carried into my own work with children. Therapy isn't something that should ever be forced. Even with the gentlest of intentions, it can create pressure. As counsellors, we can attempt to build the therapeutic relationship and foster a sense of safety for the child to feel that they can open up. But fundamentally, that decision lies with them, if they want to talk and if they are ready to talk.

I didn't feel safe with my counsellor. Through absolutely no fault of her own, I just wasn't ready, which ultimately led me to dread those sessions. I can't recall any of our exact conversations as the counselling took place, but I remember the feeling. The discomfort and uneasiness. I didn't know what to say. I didn't know what I was supposed to say. I didn't know how I felt. And honestly, I didn't *want* to know.

As adults, we must respect a child's autonomy. If a child feels forced or misunderstood, they may be put off therapy for years, even into adulthood, because they will remember how it felt for them in that counselling room, uncomfortable. And this doesn't apply only to grieving children. Children who are experiencing any type of trauma or emotional difficulties.

At the time, I was still in denial. I wasn't ready to grieve or talk about it. I don't remember crying a lot about my dad's death as a child, but the times when I did, it was always in private. In my bedroom, alone with no one to ask questions and no one around to see that I was sad.

And now, with the benefit of perspective and my counselling and psychology training, I can look back and trace parts of my journey through the **Grief Cycle**. The Grief Cycle notes the 5 stages of grief we experience throughout the bereavement process. These stages are Denial, Anger, Bargaining, Depression and Acceptance.

The Grief Cycle **(Kübler-Ross, 1969):**

- **Denial** – Feeling numb. Carrying on as if nothing has happened.
  This was me, for years. I didn't acknowledge that my life had changed. That I was grieving. That my family would never be the same. That we had suffered a tremendous loss. I wanted to pretend everything was ok when really, we had experienced a traumatic, life-altering event.
- **Anger** – Directed at ourselves, others, or the world.
  I didn't feel anger as a child, as far as I can recall, but it surfaced in my late teens/twenties. I was angry at how unfair life was. Why was *our* dad taken? A good man, gone too soon and too young, while others who had caused harm in the world lived on. How was that fair? Why him? Anger that we had been robbed of a dad, husband, son, brother, friend, neighbour. A decent, respectable and hardworking man.
- **Bargaining** – The "what ifs".
  Even now, I catch myself wondering how things might have turned out differently. If Dad had not passed away from this horrible disease, would my siblings and I be on the same path we are now? Would I have become a counsellor? Would I have met my husband?

Would I have travelled? Maybe not. That loss shaped my siblings and me, and carved out the people we have become today.

- **Depression** – A deep sadness and longing for things to be different.

  This doesn't mean a diagnosis of clinical depression, but it's heavy. A sadness that lingers. Memories that sting. Sometimes everything feels okay, until suddenly, it doesn't. It hits you like a wave. A song, a photo, a moment can suddenly bring everything back unexpectedly. When you feel like you are doing well and gaining some sort of clarity and hope for the future and for your healing, then all of a sudden, you're back to where you were.

  I remember my dad playing the song *Going Underground* by The Jam, dancing with me in our living room. For a while, that song made me unbearably sad whenever I heard it because it brought me back to that time. A time when we were happy, when dad wasn't ill, when everything was normal. But now, I love to hear that song because it reminds me of him and gives me a glimpse into the person he was. There aren't many memories like that, because we were all so young when he passed.

  My brother remembers very little of it; he was too young when my dad died. And that is a different kind of sadness altogether.

- **Acceptance** – Gradually, the pain starts to ease. Not "getting over it" by any means, but learning to live with it.

> It took me a long time to visit this stage, because it took me so long to process it. I was probably in my 20s when I could begin to accept what had happened. I finally reached a place where I could acknowledge that it was a terrible thing that happened to us during our childhood, and it's ok to feel sad about that. My counselling and psychology training helped massively with this. We weave in and out of this stage, and that's ok too. Acceptance isn't a destination. It's a state we visit, leave, and return to, like all the stages of the cycle.

This is only a brief overview of one theory of bereavement. But it is one that can help us make sense of the emotions we often struggle to name during the grieving process. There are a lot more details that could be added, and if it's something you are interested in looking into, please do. It is important when we look at the grief cycle that we remember that this is not a linear process. We do not start in denial, work our way through each stage, then reach acceptance and then suddenly feel ok. We can move through these stages in phases. We may start with denial, jump to the depression stage, back to denial, throw in some anger and then feel we have reached acceptance, then all of a sudden, we find ourselves back at depression or bargaining. All of it is ok.

Grief and bereavement are personal. No two people act or feel the same way when experiencing a loss. We all process things differently, and with that in mind, it is important that we do not compare our journey through grief with someone else's.

The biggest lesson I have learned is that grief comes in waves. Some days we feel ok, others we want to lie in bed and hide from the world. The most important thing is that we allow ourselves to feel, to experience the uncomfortable emotions and that we feel supported while doing so. This aids our acceptance and allows us to begin our healing journey.

Taking us back to my mum supporting me by getting me a counsellor in childhood (when I didn't really want to talk to one). I remember being at my dad's funeral. Standing in the Chapel next to my cousin, in the row behind my mum, when all of a sudden, a wave of sickness came over me. I tried to distract myself and thought it would soon pass, but it didn't. I felt sick, and it wasn't going away. I was scared I was going to be sick in front of everyone standing in the busy chapel. I tapped mum on the shoulder to say I was going to be sick, but my auntie, who had her arm around her at the time, turned around to us and asked my cousin to take me to go and stand outside for some fresh air. So, we stood outside for the full service. Often, I have regretted that, feeling like I should have been in there in the chapel, as technically I missed the full funeral. But ultimately, that was my body and brain protecting me, telling me that was all I could handle at that moment. I couldn't be in there. I couldn't face it.

I remember as we stood outside, my counsellor drove past me in her car and looked out at me and smiled. I had this feeling of unease come over me. As I am reflecting now, all these emotions come up that I can identify as an adult, but couldn't as a child. That encounter layered another emotion onto an already complex day. I didn't see her again after that. I told mum I didn't want to.

I remember my schoolteacher and my sister's teacher being there at the funeral, and they came to hug us after the service. I remember hiding behind my cousin because I was embarrassed. I didn't want to see them. Showing that I was shy, but also, maybe upon reflection, that I didn't want anyone at school to know what was going on. Would they treat me differently? Would they feel sorry for me? Did I want them to? All these thoughts and unanswered questions for my little 9-year-old brain. Maybe school was another form of 'escape' for me at that time. Escape from the sadness and changes at home. Where I could see my friends, do my work and try to feel some sense of normality. Maybe there was a part of me that wanted to keep the two separate.

The weeks and months after the funeral, I didn't go to my dad's grave, ever. I just couldn't face it. That would make it all seem real. So, I continued with my daily life as I usually would. Going to school, seeing friends, seeing family, playing 'The Sims' on our computer, listening to pop music and attending my Irish dancing classes. Speaking of which, this was a great focus for me at the time. I put all of my effort and concentration into Irish dancing, and it showed. When it came to competitions, I always left with first-place trophies and medals. I loved it. The focus on dancing would have been a positive distraction for me at the time. A hobby to put all of my energy into.

Distractions can be a good thing sometimes when we are going through difficult emotions. If it is a hobby or interest, or something that makes us feel physically and emotionally healthy, then I am all for distractions during your grieving process. Like exercise, focusing on healthy habits, reading, and listening to music that makes us feel good. If they are paired with a balance of allowing yourself space to feel. But sometimes we create negative forms of distraction to avoid facing reality. Such as 'doom scrolling' through social media, excessive gaming, unhealthy habits, and constantly keeping busy to avoid our thoughts or feelings around what has happened. These distractions are not productive and can have a much more negative impact on our mental health and emotional state. Especially during a time of grief and bereavement. They might distract us for a short time, but when we stop the distraction activity, our thoughts and feelings come back to bite us, harder than before. This can create a cycle of addiction, which is a whole other topic, I won't get into here, but it is important to be aware of our habits during these emotional times and ask ourselves, "Is this serving me?"

I put off going to visit my dad's grave for probably about a year or more until curiosity got the better of me, and I finally plucked up the courage to go. Of course, my gran came with me, she was my best friend and biggest supporter who would do anything for her grandchildren. I remember mum driving us to the cemetery and my prominent feeling of nervousness on that car journey. I felt sick again. I am now able to identify a lot of childhood anxiety as I reflect on this period. Something I had never previously related to my childhood. But understandable given what I had experienced. As I recollect my experiences now, that feeling comes rushing back to me, and I am transported back to that time. 25 years later, I can still remember it so clearly. Feeling sick and nervous all the time. Classic symptoms of anxiety.

As we arrived at the cemetery, we were parked on a hill with the car facing downwards. When my gran went to step out of the front seat of the car, she tripped over her handbag strap, fell, and started rolling down the hill! This was such a funny, unexpected moment, I couldn't stop laughing. Exactly what I needed in that moment to ease the tension I had built up.

Visiting the grave was not as bad as I had made it out in my head to be, but it is hard to describe what it did feel like. Sad, shock, heavy, disbelief, worry, wonder? I remember that 10-year-old girl, standing staring at the gravestone, looking at the date that he passed away. That date stuck in my head so vividly.

I recall wondering: *Is he really in there? Or is he in heaven?*

So many questions that children carry but never ask. The innocence of it all.

That visit felt like climbing a mountain. It felt like I had overcome a scary obstacle that day. But I didn't go back to the cemetery, not for years.

Childhood grief is often quiet. It doesn't always look like sadness. Sometimes it hides in writings or drawings, in silence, in acting out, or in pretending nothing happened at all. As children, we grieve with the emotional tools we have (or don't have). Tools that are still forming. We don't always have the words, so we express them in other ways, often unnoticed. A behaviour, for example.

I read recently something that said, "Grief is love with nowhere to go." If that is true, even for us as adults, then how do we expect children to experience this kind of loss and cope with it? That love for a parent, taken away with limited understanding and knowledge of what is going on, and having to navigate that through their developing years.

Looking back, I now see how my younger self was trying to make sense of something far too big for a child to understand. Grieving as a child doesn't end when we grow up, either. Often, we carry that grief with us into adulthood, where we can finally begin to name it, understand it, and tend to it with care. That's part of why I do this work now, because I know what it's like to hurt in silence, and I know the healing that can come from just simply being truly heard. Whether that is through words or actions.

We can't protect children from grief, but we *can* walk alongside them in it. We can offer patience, understanding, and gentle presence. And sometimes, that's enough. Sometimes, that's everything.

The Impact of Support Systems

When our dad died, everything familiar changed. The world felt suddenly uncertain, and the structure of our family, once held together by two parents, rested entirely on my mum's shoulders. Suddenly, she had three children under the age of 10 to support emotionally, physically and financially. Three children, too young to understand the permanence of death yet old enough to feel the ache of dad's absence.

In those early years, Mum became our world. Guiding us through the path that none of us had chosen but suddenly had to adapt to, all while she was carrying her own grief. We were extremely close to her before, of course, but after dad died, that closeness intensified. She was our everything. Even in her own heartbreak, she managed to create a sense of safety around us. An everyday hero who packed lunches, made dinners, read stories, kept the house clean and tidy, brushed hair and tried to keep life moving forward. Looking back, it amazes me how she carried all three of us while navigating her own bereavement. She had to be mother and father, caregiver and comforter, disciplinarian and friend.

We learned very early on to look out for one another. Sibling bonds became tighter through shared memories and shared loss. Yes, we still argued as siblings do, but that protectiveness for each other grew stronger.

But mum was the centre. She made us strong - not in the way people imagine strength, all toughness and resilience, but in a quiet, enduring way. Strength that shows up in daily routine. Even as children, we watched her closely, how she kept going, how she laughed, how she hardly ever let us see her cry (if ever) and how everything she did was for us and in the absence of our dad, that love became the thread that held our little family together. And she did a fantastic job!

Years later, I could still feel that closeness. It shaped the person I am today, how I love and how I hold others in their grief. Losing our dad could have shattered us. Well, in some ways it did, but in others it bound us closer to mum, to each other and the understanding that love and sadness can coexist together.

We were very lucky to have my mum's family. They were a close-knit family of 4. My Mum, her younger brother Barry (our uncle) and her Mum and Dad (our Gran and Pap). We were so close with our Gran and Pap, we used to stay over at their house every weekend from very early childhood, and sometimes they would stay at ours. I was very close to my gran in particular. Even when I was very young. I would cry whenever I left her.

Up until I was around 6 or 7 years old, they lived in a house with a beautiful big cherry blossom tree in their front garden. I was a child who absolutely loved dolls and had a huge collection. Some that stayed at my Gran Floyd's house, some that stayed at my Gran Anderson's house and some that stayed at my house and the favourites that would go with me wherever I went.

During the summer months, Gran and I would take my dolls outside and play with them in the sun, underneath the big cherry blossom tree. This tree soon gained the name 'The Dolly Tree'. A very early childhood memory I hold close to my heart.

They moved to a flat soon after Christopher was born, and 'The Dolly Tree' was no more. We drove up one day to see it, but upon our arrival, we found the new owners of the house had cut the tree down, much to our disappointment.

As I grew older, this memory seemed to fade, and I forgot all about 'The Dolly Tree' until one day, Gran reminded me of it. She told me

"I would love you to write a book about 'The Dolly Tree'",

I never got around to doing this, unfortunately. And so, to honour her request, I found it fitting to add it to this chapter.

Gran was my favourite person in the whole world. I loved spending time with her.

I vividly recall one day when I was around 8 or 9 years old, at the time when dad was ill, she was cuddling me and told me,

"You know we'll always be here for you, whatever happens."

My heart skipped a beat when I heard those words. That instantly told me something was wrong. At the time, I didn't understand the weight of those words, but it set off an alarm bell in me. Even at the age of 8/9 years old. I knew something was coming, and as the reality of my dad's illness set in, they started to make sense. When I mentioned this to her years later, she told me she didn't remember saying that. Funny how certain things stick with us. Even the small, passing moments can have a massive impact and shape the way we feel.

Uncle Barry was living in Australia at the time when my dad got ill, but he and my Auntie Lisa came home to Scotland around the time he passed away. We were really close with them too, and as we got older, we stopped staying at Gran and Pap's as much and started staying at Barry and Lisa's house at the weekends instead, which we loved. Their friends would come over, and we loved to be involved. It was always a lot of fun. We would get takeaways or walk to the shop and buy sweets and watch movies. It was always a great time. They joked and made us laugh and feel safe in a way that allowed us to forget, even if just for a moment, the weight of our grief.

We also had our friends the McPhees, who were like family to us, and as previously mentioned, must have been a great help to my mum, taking us overnight and on days out.

And we also had my dad's family, who all lived slightly further away, so we maybe saw them a bit less. But loved visiting them, and still do. We would go to stay with my dad's brothers in Stirling and Aviemore, which we loved. It helped us feel close to him even in his absence.

And of course, my Gran Anderson, dad's mum. She was around 80 years old when Dad passed away. The loveliest woman ever to grace this earth. She was deeply religious, and her home had a quieter, more structured feel than Gran Floyd's, but we loved it all the same. I often wonder what it felt like for her. To lose her youngest son when he was only 39 years old, and for his brothers and sisters to lose their youngest brother. Grief ripples through generations in different ways. Although it was never really spoken about.

While every child's experience is unique, the absence of a father or father figure can have significant consequences affecting a child's emotional, psychological, and social development. Dads often play a vital role in their child's upbringing and in shaping their sense of self and safety.

From a professional perspective, research often points to support systems being made up of therapists, teachers, counsellors, and other helping professionals as crucial to a grieving child's wellbeing. And that's absolutely true; these services can be a lifeline for many families. It's part of my job now, and I love the work I do.

But in my own experience, the most important support didn't come from professionals. It came from our friends and family.

Our Uncle Barry, in particular, became really involved and became like a 'surrogate dad' to us. Between him and my Pap, we had 2 great father figures who would do anything for us. I remember sitting in Barry and Lisa's house on the sofa with Barry when I was around 12 or 13 years old and asking him if he would walk me down the aisle on my wedding day when I grew up, and he said,

"Of Course I'm doing it. I would be offended if you asked anyone else!"

Moments like that mattered deeply. Of course, they could never replace our dad, but having those figures in our lives made all the difference. Especially for my younger brother, Christopher, who was so young when Dad passed away.

As I grew into my role as a counsellor, I began to understand more about why this mattered. Why it was important that we had those father figures in our lives, and the impact it would have on us.

John Bowlby's **Attachment Theory** explores the significance of emotional bonds between a child and their caregiver. When this bond is broken or disrupted, it can lead to long-term psychological and emotional effects, particularly in relationships with others, even into adulthood.

According to Bowlby, the two main attachment styles are Secure Attachment and Insecure Attachment. A secure attachment is created when a caregiver is responsive and predictable in meeting the child's needs by being consistent and nurturing. Creating space for the child to feel safe, secure, loved and supported.

Insecure attachment may form when the caregiver provides inconsistent care, is emotionally unavailable, is abusive or neglectful or if the child experiences a traumatic event (if their caregiver becomes seriously ill, is in a traumatic accident or passes away). The trauma and stress of losing an attachment figure can lead to deactivation of the attachment system, resulting in difficulty forming relationships in future. Children with insecure attachment might display behaviours such as:

- Becoming distressed when alone
- Rejecting others' efforts to connect or soothe them
- Appearing withdrawn, angry, or depressed
- Lacking interest in play or exploration

As they grow, these difficulties can manifest in adulthood as:

- Struggles to ask for help
- Trouble forming close relationships
- Difficulty concentrating or self-soothing
- Emotional outbursts without a clear cause
- Hyperactivity or frequent daydreaming

From my personal perspective, I think this early loss shaped me in a very specific way. I recognise themes of 'Insecure Attachment' in myself and my relationships with others as I matured. I became extremely independent. Even now, I like doing things by myself, for myself. I don't like being told what to do, and when I feel pressured or controlled, I tend to shut down. I need to spend a lot of time alone to help me process things and make sense of my emotions.

That's why the support we received from our grandparents and Uncle Barry was so important. They stepped in with affection, compassion, kindness, care, fun and most of all, *presence*.

When I reflect on how we were treated during that time, I feel an immense sense of gratitude. They showed up for us, consistently and without question. They made us feel loved and safe at a time when our world had turned upside down.

We were truly lucky to have them.

The Second Wave

During my late teen years and early 20s, I adopted a sense of 'You Only Live Once'.

This attitude perhaps derives from my dad passing away so young, and a realisation that we only have one shot at life. Life is too short to put things off; you never know what's around the corner for any of us, and so we should do what brings us joy while we can without delaying and waiting for the perfect moment. We need to experience the world and new adventures whenever we can. And with this outlook, I decided to do some travelling.

After dad died, we began spending every New Year on holiday in Tenerife with my mum, their close friends Lorraine and Joe, and a wider crowd of family and friends. We absolutely loved it. As we grew older, we started to bring our friends along on the holiday, and one year, my boyfriend (now husband) Ian came too. We looked forward to that holiday every year.

I remember around the age of 17, when we were there on holiday, saying, ***"I'm going to move here one day."***

No one took me seriously. They would all laugh and say, ***"Yeah, yeah! Everyone thinks that when they don't want to go home from a holiday."***

But I remember it so clearly as being something I desperately wanted to do.

When I was 21, I moved out of my mum's house and into my own flat. During this time, I remember thinking: *I want to travel and see the world. Life is far too short to spend in one place. I need to live life to the fullest.*

So, I planned my first journey, a solo trip to Ireland. My favourite place in the world. I can't explain it, but whenever I travel to Ireland, it feels like home. Maybe because my Pap was from Belfast.

So, I planned my trip meticulously to fly from Glasgow to Belfast, travel to Dublin, then Cork, then Galway, and finally back to Belfast to fly home to Glasgow again. All the while staying in hostels and travelling the country by train. I had it all planned to perfection. The train times and routes, how I would spend my time in each city and stopping off for a visit with my mum and dad's friends while in Cork, which was so lovely.

That trip was so empowering, I loved every second of it. Staying in hostels and meeting people from all over the world. Doing what I wanted to do, when I wanted to do it. It was so freeing. I was so proud of myself. As previously mentioned, I'm quite a quiet person by nature, and I don't think anyone in my family expected me to take on a trip like that alone. But I did, and I loved it! I'd do it again in a heartbeat.

When I got home, I realised that I loved solo travel so much that I was finally going to bite the bullet and do what I'd always said I would do. Move to Tenerife.

I researched and came across a company that, after you paid a fee, would set you up with an apartment for a month and help you get into work. It was a no-brainer for me. It was the helping hand I needed to get started in Tenerife, and if I didn't like it, I could just come home. So, I booked to go in December 2013 for a month. Just to try it out.

As Bon Jovi says, **"Who says you can't go home?"** (His 'Greatest Hits' album was my 'live your life' inspiration during this period!)

When I arrived in Tenerife, I was in an apartment with four people I'd never met, which was daunting. But we quickly got to know each other.

I ended up getting a job on Veronica's Strip, taking pictures for holiday makers in the various nightclubs and turning them into keyrings or printed photographs for people to buy as a souvenir from their holiday. I have no idea if this is still a thing, as I assume social media has taken over for storing holiday memories. But at the time, I loved it. I worked hard and made great money in the process.

When my month was up, I was devastated. I felt like I was just starting to settle into these new surroundings and this new working life. I wanted to stay longer, but I had to go home to sort out my rented flat, and I was due to start a new job at a call centre the following Monday.

When I returned to Scotland, it was a shock to the system! Not only the drastic change in weather, but in Tenerife, my working day started at 10 pm and finished at 4 am. Then coming straight back to Scotland and setting an alarm for 6 am to get up, get ready for work and get a bus to Glasgow to start your working day, that took some getting used to. I think during my first week of training, I actually fell asleep on the job! My body clock was all over the place.

But I had already booked to go back to Tenerife that coming April. This time with a one-way ticket.

So, I worked two jobs, gave up my flat, moved in with my Gran and Pap for a few months and saved as much money as I could and then left for Tenerife again. This time I stayed for 2 years. I met the best friends and had the absolute experience of a lifetime. I ended up getting a job in an Irish bar, 'The Chieftain', where I met the best people and absolutely loved it.

I had been enjoying my time in Tenerife and the new life I'd built there when, in January, Lorraine and Joe were in Tenerife for a holiday like they usually were at that time of year and had texted me to go and meet them on my night off from work. I was looking forward to seeing them. That evening, I got ready and made my way over to Los Cristianos, just like old times.

I met them at one of the local bars, and while I was there, I said to Lorraine, ***"We'll need to phone my mum tonight and speak to her while we're together."***

I picked up my phone and saw a missed call from mum. How strange! I stepped outside, where it was quieter and called her back.

"That's so weird," **I said.** ***"I was just about to phone you; I'm here with Lorraine and Joe"***

Silence.

"I've got some bad news," mum said.

My heart sank.

"Barry has died."

I couldn't comprehend what she was saying. Of all the sentences I thought might come next, this was the last thing I was expecting her to say. I remember just walking in circles outside the bar, asking her -

"What do you mean?"

I had no idea how to process it. A million things were flying through my head, none of which made sense.

That night is a blur. I remember calling my best friend Kirsty, still in shock, still pacing in circles. I was numb.

It wasn't until I got back to my apartment that it really hit me. I cried uncontrollably. I spoke to Lisa. I couldn't stop thinking about their two little girls, my cousins, Mollie and Ruby, who were only seven and five at the time. Were they ok? How would this affect them? I knew from my own childhood how devastating losing a parent is.

What about my Gran and Pap? How were they coping with the shock of unexpectedly losing their son? I wanted to see them, and I felt so far away.

How could this be happening again, not only my dad, but now my 'surrogate dad'? Another gone far too soon and too young. These were the thoughts floating around my head.

Grief is so complex. The sudden shock was overwhelming. But there was also guilt. Guilt for not being with my family, for being in another country, for missing those final weeks. Time I'd now never get back.

I went in to work the next day and told them what had happened,

***"I need to go home. I need to see my family"*, I told them.**

They were so supportive. I remember my boss, Steve, sitting with me at the internet café across the road, helping me book my flight, trying to get me home to my family as quickly as we could. My Pap paid for my last-minute flight home, as I didn't have enough money saved for something so unexpected.

Then the next day, I got another call from my sister -

"Pap's in hospital. You need to come home right now."

Surely not.

Due to the shock of losing his son unexpectedly, Pap (who had already had a heart bypass 20 years previously) had not one, not two, but **eight** heart attacks in the same day.

He'd had a pacemaker fitted years earlier, and he described what happened as "feeling like he was being shot."

It happened while he was standing in his bedroom; the force of it kept knocking him backwards onto the bed. When he was admitted to the hospital, the nurses checked the pacemaker's readings, and they confirmed that it had restarted his heart eight times. That intense sensation he described as 'being shot' was actually the pacemaker jolting his heart back to life again and again. He was in his late 70s. The shock of losing a child suddenly and unexpectedly was just too much.

But, and don't ask me how, he survived.

We had Barry's funeral, and I couldn't believe how many people turned up. The chapel was so crowded, with people even standing outside because they couldn't get through the door; it was so busy. He really was the funniest, most popular guy we ever had the pleasure of knowing. He would do anything for anyone, especially his family. He was a real character. He was very well-known and loved, and it was shown on this day by the tremendous turnout.

After a few weeks at home, it was time to return to Tenerife. I felt so conflicted. Should I stay in Scotland, or go back? I loved my life there, and true to form, if I'm honest, I wanted to escape. Just like when I lost my dad, my instinct was to get out of there. Distract myself from the shock and the heavy emotions. If I could be somewhere far away, in a place where no one knew my family, maybe I could forget. Again. If I pretend everything is normal, maybe it will be.

But this time, the guilt was stronger. I knew I should be with my family. We had just learned how quickly life can vanish. I should be with my grandparents; they were getting older. Time was precious.

I lasted a few more months in Tenerife and then booked a flight to come home for good.

It was clear when I came home that no one in my family would ever be the same again. Things felt different. There was, and still is, a big hole in our hearts from losing such a big character and a big part of all of our lives.

I was sitting with Gran and Pap one day in their house. They were talking about getting older, and Pap said, ***"I want to live to be 100 years old."***

Gran replied, ***"Don't be silly. Why would you want to live to that age?"***

He said, ***"So I can walk my four Granddaughters down the aisle when they get married."***

My heart breaks whenever I think of him saying that. His 5 Grandchildren - all fatherless in childhood.

It was clear my mum took the unexpected passing of her baby brother really hard. As did we all. He was the life and soul of not only the party but any room he walked into. The funniest guy on the planet. My gran started to go downhill too. We noticed her memory was getting bad but initially put this down to a combination of shock, grief & ageing. We later discovered that this was the early stages of dementia.

As I had moved back to Scotland, now it was time to get my life together and 'become an adult'. I decided it was the right time for me to go to college and study counselling.

The counselling course was so enlightening for me. It wasn't just theory; it was helpful with self-awareness, reflection, and personal development. I learned a lot about myself during this time. I remember doing triad work where three people rotate in roleplay as a counsellor, client, and observer as we practised our counselling skills. When it was my turn to play the role of the client, I was told I could either speak about a real-life, personal experience or I could make a story up. I didn't know what to make up, so I told them about losing my dad and Uncle Barry. The lecturer actually thought it was a made-up story because I showed little to no emotion when telling it.

I remember the others debating, and one said, ***"Well, essentially she's lost two Dads."***

That sentence **hit home**. I've never forgotten it. It was true.

It's hard for me to express how much that course changed my life. When I initially started my counselling training, I believed I was there to learn how to help others. I never imagined the work would involve looking at parts of me I had carefully avoided up until that point. I learned that healing doesn't come from avoiding pain, but by allowing it to be and meeting it with softness and compassion. I discovered that vulnerability is not a weakness to be corrected but a human experience. Perhaps even a superpower. It takes strength to allow ourselves to be vulnerable.

The course challenged me to break my beliefs about who I thought I needed to be. Strong, composed, unbreakable. I began to see things differently and see myself differently, too. I began to understand that strength is found in honesty and authenticity – in acknowledging pain, in asking for support when it is needed and allowing myself to be seen. Not feeling like I need to hide my emotions or pretend everything is ok when it's not.

I learned to listen, and as I learned to sit with the pain of others, I finally found myself able to sit with my own. Counselling didn't just give me the skills to support others; it helped me get back to myself.

After graduating from college, I was accepted into Glasgow Caledonian University, where I got my BSc (Hons) Applied Psychology (Counselling).

During my first year of University, Pap had a stroke. We went to the hospital to see him as soon as possible. He couldn't speak, but his personality was still there. I remember so clearly that we were all standing around his hospital bed. It was terrifying. This big, strong, Irish patriarch is suddenly frail and vulnerable. A sight we never imagined we would see.

About an hour after we left the hospital that night, he passed away.

I think he had waited for us to leave. I think he knew what was coming and didn't want us to see it.

This was my first loss after starting my counselling course, and although you know the theory and the ways to help manage the loss, it doesn't make it any easier to cope with.

Pap was the ultimate gentleman. He had his routine every day of getting up, having breakfast (while also making my grans for her too!), getting himself washed and ready, and he would head out to pick up the morning newspapers. At lunchtime, he would head towards the shops, stopping in at the bookies to put a bet on the horses and stopping in at his local(s) for a few "half and a half's" (which is a half pint of lager and a measure of whiskey) on his way home. Then he would make dinner for him and my gran, and they would watch TV together at night. Often, he would head into the bedroom to watch something else on the small TV when it was time for my gran to watch the soap operas! She liked to watch them "in peace," as she used to say.

My gran was his world. He did everything for her and would do anything to make her happy. He really was one of a kind. He loved his family more than anything. He would do anything for his children and his grandchildren.

When the three of us stayed with them, it would be a bit of a squeeze in their one-bedroom flat. We had makeshift beds out of old sofa cushions at each side of their bed. We loved it. In the mornings, Pap would make us a big breakfast on the same plate that we would all grab a fork and eat together. Then they would take us swimming, or we would get the bus into Paisley with my gran and auntie Mary for a walk around the shops, stopping off for a cup of tea somewhere.

We had lost someone incredibly special. The head of the family (in his own words).

Another father figure gone. By my mid-20s, I had lost three.

It is hard to put into words what it means to lose yet another person who took on that role in our lives. Each one of them shaped who I am in different ways, and this loss, although heavy in its own right, reopened a lot of old grieving wounds. It is a strange and powerful thing to mourn that role over and over at such a young age.

But I am so grateful that we had these men in our lives. Their care, presence and belief in us mattered. It still does, and I will carry them with me always. On my wedding day, I tied a charm to my Bridal bouquet with three tiny pictures. One each of my Dad, Pap and Barry, so they were all with me, walking down the aisle, just like they had said they would.

Our biggest worry now was 'How would Gran be, living on her own?'

The night Pap passed away, I stayed with my Gran so that she wasn't alone. We drank red wine and watched the movie *Chicago* - the only DVD I could find in the house. But we both loved it, so it was actually really nice to just sit and talk and just be together. I definitely get my love of musicals from her. I stayed in bed with her, just like when I was a child.

I couldn't help but notice the role reversal. I was looking after her, the way she had for me. I feel that is a type of grief in its own right, too. Grieving how life looked previously, grieving the person that they used to be.

That same year, my Gran Anderson also passed away. She wasn't far away from her 98th birthday. Absolutely incredible. And she was amazing for her age, too. Even in her early 90s, she would still be going round and looking after her friends and neighbours who needed help. Many who were much younger than she was. She really was the most amazing and caring lady.

She taught me how to knit, how to sow and cross stitch. I remember once making a picture of a bear through a cross-stitch activity that she helped me complete. If I remember correctly, it was framed and kept in her house. She must have been proud of my one and only craft project!

As time passed by, Gran's (Floyd) dementia worsened. After a while, we had to get carers to come to her home several times a day to help her, and then it got to the stage where she had to move into a local care home. It was tough for all of us, but it was the right decision. She could no longer look after herself at home.

While clearing out my Gran and Pap's flat after she had moved, this was where I found everything she had kept of mine, my siblings and my cousins over the years. All my jotters from as far back as primary school, the cards I had made for my dad when he was in hospital, stories I had written, and pictures we had drawn. I love her so much for keeping these things because finding them brought back so much nostalgia and memories I didn't know I had.

On Christmas Eve 2022, Ian and I had taken my friend Danielle's 4-year-old twins out for the day. We were giving Danielle and Scott some time to wrap presents and get things organised for the kids for Christmas Day.

We took the kids to see Santa and then stopped off at a café. As we sat down at the table in the café, ready to order, my phone rang. It was Mum. I thought, *I'll call her back.*

Then Ian's phone rang. He stepped outside to answer and then came back in and said:

"I think you'd better call your Mum."

So I did. I went outside to return her phone call, and then she told me.

Gran had passed away.

My childhood best friend. My biggest supporter.

She would do anything for her grandchildren and let us get away with things our mum definitely wouldn't! She understood me in a way few others ever have. We were so alike, she always used to say that. And I'm so glad we were.

I miss her terribly. I miss her singing when she leaves the room - which, I've noticed, I do too.

I miss her stories, her quirks and her presence. I miss all of them a lot. We all do.

Losing someone is always hard. But on Christmas Eve, when everything is supposed to be joyful, it was devastating. We woke up the next morning still in shock, still in limbo. Nothing could be done over the holidays. No funeral arrangements. Just... waiting. But we headed over to my mum's house for Christmas

Day as we usually would and had already planned to do. But we didn't feel much like celebrating.

It was a hard pill to swallow.

I think about them daily and wish I could tell them things about life and fill them in on what's been happening. I wore my gran's gold ring on my wedding day as my 'Something Old' and still wear it now. I had an orchestral version of 'Beauty and the Beast' playing as my Bridesmaids walked down the aisle. This was Gran's (and my) favourite Disney film, and we used to watch it together all the time when I was young.

I remember back to those days when my siblings and I would go and stay with them at weekends during childhood, and I was told I could bring a video to watch; I would always bring Beauty and the Beast for me and Gran to watch together. Or sometimes 'The Jungle Book', as that was Pap's favourite. He liked Louis Prima, who voiced 'King Louis', the orangutan. I used to alternate which one I brought. I loved both those films and wanted to bring something for them to enjoy also. (I have always been a people pleaser, even as a child!)

In seven years, we had lost nearly all of our family.

My mum's whole immediate family, apart from her children, were gone.

This is a lot of bereavement for anyone to carry. Especially at a young age.

But nothing or no one could prepare us for what was coming next.

The Tidal Wave

I remember the few days leading up to this like it was yesterday.

Saturday 10th August 2024 - my friends and I, along with their kids and their mums, had booked tickets to *The Foodies Festival* in Glasgow. There were live music performances, food and drink stalls, and a great atmosphere. I'd spoken to mum the night before, asking if she wanted to join us, but she said,

"No, I'm not feeling up to it; that would be too much walking for me just now. I'll be feeling better in a few weeks."

She had fallen the year before, breaking three bones in her neck. She spent months in the hospital and was then bed-bound in a neck brace for months at home afterwards. Luckily, she healed enough that it came off just before my wedding.

So, we went to the 'foodies festival' and had a great time. I phoned mum the next day to tell her all about it.

Sunday 11th August - Ian and I had planned to do '*The Kiltwalk*' - a 20-mile trek from St Andrews to Dundee to raise money for charity with some of Ian's workmates. A great day, although very difficult! And I hadn't realised how my fitness had dropped until this point. I was quickly humbled and realised it was time for me to get back out walking and running again. Ian and I have done plenty of outdoor hiking, trekking and adventures, but I immediately learned how easily you lose your fitness when you don't keep it up and stay consistent. (Note to self!)

Monday 12th Aug – The day had finally come. My school summer holiday was over, and I was back at work. As I work in schools, I had been off for the 6-week summer holiday. Our first week after summer is always a training week in the office for all staff members before heading back into our designated schools the following week, which is lovely because we all get to see each other and catch up. Throughout the rest of the year, we are all based in different schools throughout the West of Scotland, so we all rarely get the chance to meet up. I remember this day vividly because of how sore I was; my legs were in so much pain, and I could hardly sit or stand due to the lengthy walk the day before! But with that aside, I was looking forward to catching up with my colleagues and adjusting to the working week again.

That night, I went onto our 'Family Chat', our group chat on Facebook Messenger with Mum, Louise, Christopher and myself, just after 8 pm to tell them about my first day back at work, and we were laughing about how sore my legs were and the fact that I could hardly walk.

We checked in with Christopher, who was doing 'The West Highland Way'. A 96-mile hike through the Scottish Highlands. Ian and I had done the hike before, so I knew what he was letting himself in for! I remember it had been really bad weather, including thunder and lightning, so we were checking that he was ok and how he coped camping in the storm.

I said, "I was so tired after the Kiltwalk, I slept right through it. I didn't hear any thunder at all!"

Mum said, "I never heard a thing either!"

Tuesday 13th August.

I arrived at the office and noticed a few missed calls from Mum's partner, Robert. At first, I assumed he'd dialled me by mistake as his daughter is also called Heather and there is no reason why he would be phoning me at 8.30 am. But as I sat down at the table with colleagues, about to make a coffee and start the day, he called again. I excused myself from the room and answered the call.

That life-altering call that would change everything.

"Heather... It's your mum." A brief pause. **"She's died."**

In that very second, my entire world collapsed.

No warning. No time to prepare.

There are no words for what goes through your head in that moment. Nothing. Just blankness. Shock. Confusion. Disbelief. But mainly shock.

"I was just talking to her last night. What do you mean?" I said. **"I need to go."**

I wandered around the building aimlessly for a few minutes, not sure what I was supposed to do. I found my manager and somehow managed to stutter the words through the blankness, confusion, and shock: **"My mum has just died."**

Then came the tears after I had said it out loud. Reality struck, and before I knew it, overpowering tears came, accompanied by a deep sense of panic and dread. I remember shaking a lot. She took me to a quiet room. My whole body went cold. Time slowed down. My heart pounded. I felt faint. I felt sick. I felt like I was going into shock.

I felt like I didn't know where I was. It felt like a dream. Nothing felt real.

A mix of colleagues took it in turns to sit with me, one at a time, and make sure I was ok. But I wasn't ok.

If there was ever a place to receive that kind of devastating news, being surrounded by trained counsellors was maybe a small blessing.

I just kept saying

"How has this happened?"

"I was talking to her last night."

The shock was so deep, it didn't even feel like pain. It was just silence. Numbing silence.

I eventually managed to get myself together enough to call Ian, my husband. I couldn't even say the words. Finally, through short, sharp breaths and tears, I managed: **"My mum has died."**

He dropped everything at his own work and came to collect me straight away.

I was still in a state of shock when we left the office. We drove directly to my sister Louise's house. I called my best friend Kirsty and my Auntie Lisa on the way. Lisa left her work immediately and met us at Louise's flat. I didn't even know what to say to Louise when I got there. We hugged and cried and then just sat in her living room in a shocked state of silence for a while. I remember running to her bathroom and being physically sick.

Once Lisa arrived, we sat with her for a while, and then Ian and I went to Mum's house, where Robert was. He was with his daughter, and the undertakers were also there by this point.

Trying to process the devastating news we had just received was far too much for us all. But Ian and I made that trip to Mum's house. There was a disturbing sense of dread that filled my body as we drove closer and closer to the house.

I considered seeing mum one last time before they took her away, but I couldn't bring myself to do it. We just sat there. I was still in shock. Robert's daughter stayed with him that night, and Ian and I went back to Louise's.

I tried for hours and hours to reach Christopher on the phone, but because he was trekking through the remote Highlands, he had little to no phone signal. We couldn't get a hold of him. I called him over 20 times. Eventually, he picked up, but the phone signal was poor. Imagine trying to break that news to someone over the phone with a bad reception. Ian drove to the highlands to collect him from wherever he was on the trail and brought him home to us.

Once we were all back at Louise's, the three of us hugged tightly. My sister, brother, and I.

Then we just sat. In silence, all day. Just the three of us.

Orphaned. All our parents and parental figures. Gone.

It hit hard. Horrifically hard.

The following days and weeks passed in a blur. I remember occasional visits from friends, loads of flowers arriving, and cards stacked across the living room. But that is all.

Christopher stayed at Louise's house so that neither of them was alone, and Ian and I went over to be with them every day.

My work was incredible. They gave me months off and checked in regularly. There was no way I could have returned to counselling. Holding space for others, while feeling so broken myself.

We began funeral arrangements. Dealing with banks, solicitors, and wills. All while in deep grief. But somehow, we managed. Together, we split tasks and just... got through.

No one talks about this part. The admin that comes after a death. When you are suddenly trying to just survive and make it through each day, you quickly realise you also have the responsibility of dealing with important documents and finances. It is very overwhelming, and some things we are still trying to work through over a year later. I think this is an important topic because, for an outsider looking in, it can be difficult to understand just how much your brain is in survival mode and by that, I mean just gathering the energy to try and function each day. The responsibility is really difficult to cope with on top of heavy emotions, and if you're dealing with this right now, please just know, I see you.

As Christmas approached, it was time for me to go back to work on a *phased-return basis*, two days per week, which I could just about manage.

But the holidays themselves were unbearable. Christmas had always been about family. Now it was just us three. Only the three kids left. How did this happen? Ian did his best to distract us. Planning days out, etc, which we were very grateful for. We booked to go out for Christmas dinner, something we'd never done before in our lives. It was me, Ian, Christopher, Louise, and her friend Chris. After dinner, we changed into our pyjamas and had drinks at Louise's house. Friends came by to join us. We tried to enjoy it, but none of us really felt present. I just wanted the day to be over.

Then came the New Year, something I dreaded even more.

The New Year is always hard for me with the anniversaries of Dad, Barry, Pap, and Gran's all falling in around that time of year. Mum used to hate the New Year, too. I guess that rubbed off on me.

In an attempt to get away from it all, we booked a lodge in Stirling, on the grounds of where our wedding venue was, to spend New Year's Eve away from home. We all went, along with some friends. But that morning, I couldn't stop thinking:

"I don't want to go."

My anxiety about being with others, having to smile, be sociable, and to be 'on' during the festive period... it was overwhelming.

We arrived, we unpacked, and as I went to change from my leggings and hoodie that I had travelled in, into some nicer clothes for the countdown to the next year, I realised the zip had broken on my jumpsuit I planned to wear. Meaning the only other clothes I had were my bright pink tartan, unflattering but comfortable pjs. So, everyone else was dressed up, and I had my PJs on. If anything, this made me feel worse. Don't get me wrong, I am all for being cosy in your PJs! As anyone will tell you, the second I get the opportunity, I change into my comfy clothes. But sometimes getting dressed up makes you feel good, and at that moment, I wanted to get dressed up, to make a bit of an effort to try and lift my mood and get me into the party spirit. But it didn't work out quite like that.

As the night went on and it got closer to midnight, we put the TV on as we approached *The Bells*, the New Year's Eve Scottish broadcast from Edinburgh Castle, counting down to midnight and the New Year. As soon as I heard the bagpipes, I broke. Holding in the emotion was just too much. I went to the bathroom to cry, but Louise followed and sat with me.

As midnight struck and 2025 began, we hugged tightly, just the three of us.

This was it.

Just us now.

Louise, Christopher, and I.

It was emotional. Really emotional. I cried again. It's in these little moments where it really hits.

I went to bed early that night. I had as much as I could handle and just wanted the celebrations to be over. Because I didn't feel like celebrating. I actually felt so down that night that after I went to bed and lay there alone as everyone else continued partying, I researched some local counselling organisations to put myself on some waiting lists to get my own therapy.

I knew no one would get back to me on New Year's Eve, but at least I had taken the first step to getting the help it was clear I needed.

The next day, New Year's Day, was better. It felt so much more relaxed.

We drank prosecco in the hot tub, sang karaoke, and played games. This felt like a moment of light. A nice day with family and friends to compensate for yesterday. Maybe the pressure of New Year's Eve to have fun, mixed with the raw emotions, was just too much the day before. But the 1st of January seemed less pressured somehow. That I could just be with friends and family and enjoy myself.

Once home, after the holidays had finished, I returned to work four days a week. During my bereavement leave, I had been quietly preparing to relaunch my coaching and counselling practice, *Heather Higgins Coaching*. But upon my return to both jobs, at that time in January, it was all too much too soon. I pushed too hard and hit burnout.

I was trying to adjust to working 4 days per week in schools, with some long drives to and from work, making the days longer. Seeing one-to-one clients, trying to advertise my business, and running group 'Monthly Wellbeing Challenges'. It was a lot. My thinking was -

"If I keep busy and get back to normal, everything will feel ok again."

Where have I heard that before? Oh, right! Going back to school after my dad died. And moving back to Tenerife after Barry's funeral.

On top of everything, around this time, my brother Christopher had decided to join the Royal Navy and was due to leave for his training at the same time as I was returning to work. I felt so many things: pride, fear, anxiety, helplessness.

Everyone said, **"Don't worry, it'll be great for him,"** and it was. I am so proud of him. But at that time, that pride was laced with anxieties.

I couldn't sleep; I was constantly waiting for *another* devastating phone call. After so much loss, I was now always bracing for the next. The anxiety was deep-rooted by this point. I was traumatised by the sudden shock and loss. My brain was stuck in fight or flight mode. Understandable as we were still trying to process the shock of losing our mum.

I didn't want him to go; I wanted the three of us to be near each other, where I knew they were safe. That's selfish of me, I know. He has his own life to live, and so he should.

22-year-old me would be telling him, **"You Only Live Once, so go for it!"**

When Christopher left for his training, Louise also booked a trip to travel with a friend. The day she left, I had a panic attack at work. The worst I have ever experienced. I tried to voice note my best friend, Kirsty, to speak to her, and I couldn't get the words out. I couldn't breathe. I was crying uncontrollably. The intrusive thoughts were a lot, paired with the anxiety -

"What if something happens to one of them?"

"I can't protect them."

"What if I lose them too?"

With them both away, I felt alone.

Although I know I wasn't. I had Ian and my friends, but there was something about both of them being away out of the country that made me feel so alone. It's hard to explain that feeling.

And as if that weren't enough, we were also buying a house at this time.

Ian handled everything during the process. Mortgage advisors. Banks. Packing. Moving. I truly could not have gotten through this without him.

The house we bought is located on the street right next to the one we grew up in. I can actually see our old family home from our garden as I write this.

I started a tradition that every 4th January, on the anniversary of dad's passing, I would walk past the street we grew up in and follow the walking route that dad used to take us on when we were kids. I'd imagined living back here one day. One might say I manifested it. But when it finally happened, the nostalgia was too raw. Too heavy at this time. It had been only 6 months since Mum had passed. So, at a time when I should have been happy and excited about buying a home together in a lovely area, an area I always wanted to move back to, the area I grew up in, and had lovely memories, I was just sad. It was hard.

Those lovely memories became hard to look at. I look across to that house, and I can see parts that my dad had built that still stand there today. The front garden that was renovated when we lived there, the ramp he built so that he could get his wheelbarrow up and down from the garden to his van on the street, and his shed at the side of the house. And now I was met with no option but to reminisce about these times every day when I stepped outside my house. Remembering a time when they were both here. A time when we were all happy, and life was good.

I felt a deep sense of guilt about this because I felt like I should be happy, and I could see how excited Ian was, but in all honesty, I was struggling.

Renovations soon began in our new home. A new kitchen, new flooring, and new furniture arrived and were built and moved around. For a few weeks, we lived in what resembled a building site. I couldn't relax. My happy place is my sofa, my blanket, my scented candles lit and cuddles from my rescue dog Dennis. Relaxing with Ian in our living room, watching TV. But it was unavailable during the time I needed it the most.

I could feel my mental health taking a dip and knew I needed to make some changes.

Reducing my work hours wasn't financially possible after taking on a mortgage. But I could scale back my coaching business. I paused my 'monthly challenges', which freed up several evenings of my working week. The *instant* relief that brought me was telling. My body had been screaming for rest. For me to slow down. Amongst the chaos and the stress that surrounded me, it was time to step back and start taking care of myself.

It was around this time that I also started seeing a counsellor. This helped enormously. I began reflecting on self-care and advice I'd given to my own clients, but I hadn't been following myself. I started going out for walks again, exploring the area around our new home, the same places that Dad used to take us as kids. Especially the country roads and nearby farms with horses. I had found a new happy place. A place I could go and walk in nature and clear my head.

Eventually, Christopher had his Royal Navy passing out parade at the end of his training. Ian and I made the 9-hour drive to Plymouth to be there for him. Seeing him in his uniform, knowing he was thriving, I was overwhelmed with pride. I cried proud big sister tears the whole day. He had been away for 10 weeks at this point, so seeing each other again was emotional. Ian actually caught it on video, and I love watching that moment where we reunited.

When we returned home to Scotland, I started exercising again, leaving the house more. Slowly, I began to rethink how I wanted my business to evolve. Quietly, I worked in the background without giving myself time scales and deadlines, without advertising for new clients. There was no pressure. But suddenly, things started to make sense. I was excited about relaunching my business and had lots of new ideas for services I could offer and how to structure my working week so that it worked well for me and not against me.

I learned to slow down.

To feel.

To cry when I needed to.

To honour the grief.

To finally let myself *just be*.

Small Gestures, Big Impact

"I can't imagine what you're going through."

Does that sentence sound familiar? I don't know about you, but I've heard that being said to me before.

And this is really difficult. For both the person who is grieving and the other person who perhaps feels awkward and is scared of causing upset or uncomfortable feelings in the room. So, I have found the most common way is for people to say nothing. To not mention it at all. Grief is like the elephant in the room that no one wants to acknowledge.

And sometimes that can be ok. Sometimes, as grievers, we want to go out with the girls or go for a weekend away to take our mind off things and just be ourselves for a short time again. To feel that sense of 'normality', although in reality, everything feels far from normal.

But sometimes, we *want* to talk about it. We *want* to mention them, and we *want* you to know that we are finding it difficult. We need to have that space to be allowed to feel what we are feeling without an added layer of guilt about not wanting to make *you* feel uncomfortable.

Grief is the most universal experience we will go through as humans; everyone will experience it in some shape or form, so why does it feel like such a lonely place for so many of us? Why is it still taboo for us to talk about? It should be the most talked-about thing, as it applies to us all.

If people carry on 'acting normal,' it can make someone grieving feel that they can't open up. It can make them feel like they don't want to 'bring the mood down' or make other people feel awkward or uncomfortable.

But we should be able to. We shouldn't feel like we need to keep quiet about our feelings or live in fear of talking about those who have passed.

Shout their names from the rooftops!

Speak about them often.

Keep their memory alive.

Tell stories.

Every year since her passing, a group of us get together and go out for lunch and to raise a glass on my mum's birthday, 14th Feb. Although the first year was raw and emotional, it still felt like we were doing something special to honour her and remember her. And I am still so grateful to everyone who made an effort and joined us.

This year we are doing the same again, and I hope the tradition carries on.

These are the times that matter. When people show up for you in your grief. When you feel supported and that you are not alone.

To hear stories, to laugh, to cry if you need to. The important thing is that you have that dedicated time or space to do so.

If you are in this situation, if you are a friend or family member watching someone grieve, if you are ever at a loss of what to do or say when someone is grieving, ask the person who is going through a bereavement what they would like. When you meet up for that coffee, ask if they want to use this time as an escape, or if they want to talk about their grief. It's important that they feel supported.

Understandably, people might want to shy away from the subject for fear of causing upset, but this can be misconstrued by someone going through a bereavement as people 'not caring' or lead to them thinking 'people have forgotten about me'.

Life goes on for everyone else after you have suffered a loss, and this is a hard thing to accept sometimes. Your life has been completely turned upside down, and yet everyone else is living their usual lives. And it feels awful.

Just know, if someone close to you is going through a bereavement, there is no right thing to say. There are no words you can say that will make things better for them. You can't fix it. You can't take their pain away.

So, just show up.

A text, a phone call, a visit.

Just let them know that you are thinking about them and ask what they need from you to feel supported in that moment.

And that brings us to – What Not To Say.

"Be Strong" – this is a hard one because it might feel like you are being supportive here, but sometimes, we don't need to be strong. Sometimes we want to break down and cry. And that's allowed. By telling someone to be strong, it almost makes them feel like they are not allowed to show their emotions or be sad, which is completely wrong and can bring feelings of shame on top of everything else for the griever. I remember this being said to me often as a child. Why should a 9-year-old who has just lost their parent have to be strong?

"You're an Orphan now" - Hearing it like that is a shock and often unhelpful. Sometimes we need to see the humour in it, though. And honestly, if you didn't laugh, you would cry! So sometimes we need to see the lighter side, because honestly, you couldn't make it up. But that sentence was so triggering for me personally, especially just after mums death.

"They wouldn't want you to be sad" – Again, it's understandable you want to offer some sense of comfort, but this is another statement that could easily make someone feel that their emotions are not valid and they should somehow "be stronger" or "be over it by now". This is not helpful. Missing someone who has passed is not a weakness; it is not something to be ashamed of or hidden. People are allowed to feel sad. **It is a natural human reaction to loss.**

"You need to get on with your life" – Not only does this statement invalidate someone's grief, but it also minimises the significance of their loss. It creates pressure for the person who is grieving, who may already be struggling with feelings such as guilt, confusion or fear about the future, so being told to 'move on' can feel like being told to 'perform better emotionally', making the griever feel alone and misunderstood.

"At least it was quick" – To someone who has experienced any sort of shock or trauma, this is not comforting. Because honestly, all this experience has brought is distress. There is no "at least" about it. I understand perhaps you are trying to find a moment of positivity during a devastating time, but anyone who is grieving and hears the words "at least", believe me, probably will not feel comforted.

"Are you ok?" – I think this one is pretty self-explanatory. They are not ok. They are probably the furthest from ok they have ever been. But asking this question may make them feel like they need to say 'Yes' even when they are not. I know I do.

"My {mum/dad/insert meaningful deceased person here} is doing my head in!" – Just read the room! People are, of course, allowed to feel how they feel, and maybe your mum/dad has done something to irritate you that day. Your story is your story, and you are allowed to feel how you feel, but please, do not go to your grieving friend and rant about it because they would give ANYTHING to have *their* mum/dad around to be annoying them. To have one more day to have the opportunity to say, 'My mum is doing this...' or 'My dad did this today'. It may be difficult for them to offer a sympathetic ear because, in their mind, "at least you still have them here."

Try to put yourself in their shoes for a second, and maybe go to one of your other friends who is not grieving that family member and talk to them about it instead. Just be mindful of the heavy emotions that will be present.

"Let me know if you need anything" – This statement will almost always be well-intentioned, but I can tell you with certainty that a griever, more often than not, will not reach out to you if they need anything. Here's why –

Grief is overwhelming. People in mourning are often emotionally, mentally, and physically drained. Asking them to *figure out what they need, find the right words*, and *reach out* adds another task to their already heavy load. Many simply won't have the capacity to ask for help, even if they truly need it.

In early grief, especially, people are just trying to survive. They might not be able to identify their needs or prioritise them. Being expected to articulate specific requests can feel impossible. Also, "anything" is so open-ended that it can feel meaningless. The grieving person might not know what "counts," or may feel unsure about whether they're asking too much of you.

If you are at a loss or confused about what to say to someone going through a bereavement, try some of these alternatives instead.

"How are you coping today?" – This is more open and invites the person to open up and think about how they are coping, rather than a simple yes/no answer.

"What kind of support do you need today?" – Again, this is more open-ended and invites the person to think about what they need and make their needs known.

"I don't have the perfect words, but I am thinking about you." – They know you can't fix it for them or say anything that will make this any easier, but letting them know you are thinking of them can often be a comfort in itself.

"Your feelings are valid, and it's ok to feel whatever it is you are feeling." – This is a great alternative to "they wouldn't want you to be sad". It lets the griever know that what they are feeling is normal and all part of the process.

"I'm here to listen, or if you don't feel like talking, I'm here to sit with you if you would like." – This is a compassionate and caring statement that gives the griever options on how they would like to be supported. Sometimes they want to talk and need someone to listen, other times they just need someone to be there and sit with them. Others may feel like they need a distraction and to talk about anything else other than their bereavement. Sometimes they need time alone. Let them tell you what they need.

Summary – please be mindful of how we speak to others who are suffering. They are delicate. They are sensitive. Of course, you are human too, and you may make mistakes. In fact, when it comes to someone you love who is grieving or suffering, you will almost certainly make mistakes. Especially if you yourself have not experienced the loss that they have. You are not a bad person. You are learning too. It's a learning curve for everybody, and there is no manual to get us through it.

There is no point in guessing what that person may need or want from you, so the best thing you can do is ask them. Communicate and make the first step to show you are there for them. Because often the griever will feel overwhelmed, sad, and be looking for who is there for them. It is not their job to reach out. They know you are busy, they know you have your own life, and they will not want to intrude. At times like this, they will remember who was there for them, who offered their support, who reached out and who didn't.

Just remember, however uncomfortable it is for you, they feel 100x more uncomfortable. It can feel hard for them to reach out, so sometimes they need you to make the first move.

Please be patient with those who are grieving. This intense emotional period will change them. You might notice that they overreact to seemingly small things (but this may have triggered them). You might notice they are more irritable, frustrated, or angry (they are carrying an overwhelming mental load). They might seemingly lose interest in things they used to enjoy or not participate in or attend things you used to do together (because they are tired of masking and pretending that they feel ok when they don't).

Please don't take these things personally. Look deeper into their behaviour and ask yourself why they might be acting this way.

They may be dealing with conflicting thoughts or needs at the same time (and if you are the one who is going through this, this is ok. It's completely natural.) They may feel that they want to be alone but also crave comfort or support. They may feel the need to hold on and keep memories alive while moving forward with life. They may feel they need to cry or talk, and then the next minute, they want to shut down and avoid the pain. They may appear that they want to manage their grief and maintain some kind of control, yet feel the need to surrender to the unpredictability of their emotions, which can't be avoided.

For me, the biggest conflict lay in wanting support, yet wanting independence, wanting loved ones close but also needing time and space by myself to grieve alone. Along with that conflict of having comfort in rituals and keeping things the same, yet having the urge to want to do new things and create new environments that reflect your life after a loss.

Sometimes, just naming these contradictions or conflicts can help reduce the pressure to "choose" one or the other.

As we can see, grief is not tidy or straightforward. Grief is messy. It's unpredictable and deeply personal. It holds paradoxes, and both sides can be true at once. And while there's no guidebook for how to navigate the awkward silences or the well-meaning but misplaced words, there *is* something simple we can all do: show up for those who are suffering a loss. Be present. Listen. Ask!

And if you're not sure what to say, say that. Because silence, when rooted in love and accompanied by presence, can say more than words ever could. But please do not avoid the people in your life who are grieving. This can make them feel unloved, unwanted, and that their trauma and grief are not welcome.

Let's stop pretending the elephant in the room isn't there; name it. Share stories, cry, laugh. Honour the person who's gone by holding space for those left behind. You don't need to fix anything. That is not your job. You just need to *be there*. Let them know they have people around them.

So, if you're wondering how to help, start by asking them.

"Do you want to talk about it?" might just be the most powerful thing you can say. And if they do, let them speak. If they don't, just keep them company. Keep inviting, keep remembering, and keep reaching out. Because in a world that too often moves on too quickly, your willingness to stay could be the greatest comfort of all.

Grief as an Unexpected Teacher

Everyone's journey through loss, grief, and bereavement is personal and different. No two people experience it the same way. This can be due to several factors, including our individual personalities, our circumstances, our past experiences, relationships, our core beliefs, attachment styles, self-awareness, or our outlook on life.

This story, my story, will probably be very different from others who have experienced bereavement, and that's okay. While there may be similarities in how people grieve, the way we process it is unique.

Between Louise, Christopher, and me, although we've experienced the same losses, we have all dealt with it differently. And there is no right or wrong way to think, feel, or act during this time.

One of the biggest lessons I've learned is that *accepting* our emotions and *acknowledging* them is essential to moving through them. **We need to feel to heal.**

And that's hard. Because our first instinct is often to distract ourselves, to keep busy and avoid the pain. I did this for years. As a child and as an adult. That wanting to escape. My body being in constant 'flight mode'. Wanting to run away. My brain working overtime to try and protect me and keep me safe. But when the distractions stop, and we're left alone with our thoughts and feelings, they hit us like an avalanche. You can only push emotions away for so long before they come back, louder and heavier.

In my role as a counsellor and coach, it's not just important, it is essential that I look after myself, in order to be able to be there for others. And this is where 'supervision' comes into play. Supervision is a requirement for counsellors, coaches and many other helping professions to maintain ethical and good practices in our work. It enhances professional development while promoting the well-being of both the counsellor and the client. If there was ever anything I felt I needed to offload or work through, or if my own experiences were affecting my work with a client, I would talk about this at my monthly supervision sessions with my supervisor.

You can't pour from an empty cup.

And that applies to everyone. Whether you're grieving or going through any challenges in life, looking after yourself is not optional; it is necessary. Your children, your siblings, your parents, your clients or friends, whoever is in your life that you show up for, they all benefit when you are well.

Fix your own oxygen mask before assisting others.

Have you ever heard that safety announcement on an aeroplane? There's a reason. If you're too busy helping someone else breathe during an emergency, you might end up starving yourself of oxygen and gasping for air yourself. Struggling so much that you end up suffocating, unable to help others or yourself.

It may sound selfish to prioritise yourself, but I promise you it is not. Ignoring your needs can lead to burnout. That's what happened to me.

When I returned to my counselling and coaching role in January after the 2025 New Year's celebrations (although it didn't feel much like a celebration to me at the time), I focused entirely on others. My own needs came last. I was dealing with trauma, shock, loneliness, anxiety, depression, and grief - while trying to run a business, work, move house, adapt to a new environment and all that moving entails, cope with change, be a wife, a sister, a friend, a dog mum, a counsellor, a coach.

Sounds exhausting, right? It was.

But I thought I could manage. I thought I could get on with life and that things would soon start to feel ok again. I was wrong.

It was around February time, about six months after mum had died, during our house move, that I really began to feel it. I was worn down. Emotionally, physically, mentally. I was masking everything with a smile, trying to hold it together for everyone else and pretending everything was ok. But my husband Ian could see things were not right.

My birthday was coming up. So was what would have been Mum's 65th birthday. My mum, gran, and I all had birthdays that fell in the same week in February. Three generations of girls born in the same month. We had planned a day out to celebrate what would have been Mum's birthday with friends and family. I was grateful for the effort people made to be there, but I remember that I had nothing left to give.

Louise and I smiled and laughed that day. We put on our brave faces and ate and drank with our friends. But it was one of the hardest days emotionally. These can often be the hardest moments. The birthdays, Christmases, anniversaries. The celebrations that they are not here for.

After that, I knew I couldn't keep going like this. I wasn't okay.

But still, when people messaged to check in and ask, "Are you ok?", I'd reply with:

"Yeah, I'm fine." or

"Up and down."

But really wanting to say **"I'm drowning, actually. This is really difficult, I'm struggling to cope."**

It was around this time that I started to hear back from some of the counselling organisations I reached out to on New Year's Eve. During those initial conversations over the phone, just that moment of **saying out loud** that I was struggling, automatically released so much pressure.

I ended up accessing counselling, which helped me process what I was going through and helped me release some of those thoughts and feelings I had been building up that soon had turned into overwhelm and eventually burnout. It helped me realise just how much I had been neglecting my own needs at a time when it should have been a priority.

One question my counsellor kept asking me was:

"What would you tell a client in your position?"

That hit hard. Because the answer was obvious: *Take care of yourself.* Something I wasn't doing. *You can't pour from an empty cup.*

Self-care is something I'm passionate about when working with clients. But it's not always candles, face masks, and bubble baths (although those are valid too, and fantastic forms of self-care if that's your thing).

It's also:

- Setting boundaries
- Saying no
- Taking a step back
- Looking after your physical health
- Knowing how to boost your own happy chemicals
- Honouring your emotions
- Self-awareness

It's expressing how you feel, whether that's through talking, journaling, creativity, or simply allowing yourself to feel.

Another huge lesson I've learned through grief is understanding what *really* matters. It helped me see the bigger picture and shift my priorities.

Things that used to stress me out, just...don't anymore.

For example, I used to be a really nervous driver. I hated unfamiliar roads. But after mum passed away, Kirsty invited me to join her family for a short break at Drimsynie, a gorgeous holiday village near the Arrochar Alps past Loch Lomond in Scotland.

I said yes.

And I drove there alone, on unfamiliar roads, past Loch Lomond and through beautiful scenery, listening to my favourite music. And I wasn't nervous. I didn't care about the roads or the drive. There were more important things on my mind, and escaping for a night sounded like exactly what I needed.

And do you know what? It was.

But maybe the *biggest* lesson grief has taught me is how much society rushes it.

There is this silent expectation to "move on" and be "back to normal" quickly, even after life-shattering events. Productivity is prioritised over processing. Sometimes that pressure comes externally, or sometimes it comes from within. Expecting too much from ourselves too soon.

I was lucky; my workplace gave me three months off and a phased return, and even with that, I still struggled. But my sister and brother had to return to work within a week or two, due to financial strain and workplace policies. If they had broken their leg, would they have been expected back at their desks in a week? Probably not.

But emotional injuries - the grief, loss, trauma, anxiety and depression- they are invisible and often treated as less valid, less important. And that needs to change.

Grief arrived in my life uninvited and broke things apart. Plans, assumptions, and the sense of safety I once carried. But in its wake, it also revealed things I never expected to learn.

Grief has taught me that love doesn't end when someone passes away. It lives on in our memories, in our thoughts, in photos and stories, in rituals (like going for a walk that Dad used to take us on), in the quiet ways we honour those we've lost.

It's shown me the strength of vulnerability, the courage it takes to keep showing up in the world, even when your heart is hurting more than anything. That we are capable of so much more than we sometimes think we are, or that we give ourselves credit for. That 'strength' doesn't mean soldiering on and getting on with things and saying 'we are fine'. That strength actually is found in allowing ourselves to acknowledge our feelings, to sit with the pain, and experience the uncomfortable emotions.

Mostly, grief has taught me about presence. How precious and fleeting time really is. It has taught me to take less for granted. To slow down and truly *feel*.

I never wanted to be a student of grief. But I can't deny what it has taught me: how to sit with pain, how to hold space for others in theirs, and how to live with more compassion, strength, and meaning.

When Hurt Meets the Helping

A lived experience of hurt and pain can create a deep sense of empathy towards others. Empathy is the ability to put yourself in someone else's shoes and view the world from their perspective, an essential skill in counselling. And with that, I take my lived experience of loss not as a positive, of course, but perhaps as something useful in being able to empathise with, support, and help others.

You may ask, "How can you help others after what you have been through yourself?" I am asked this question a lot, especially after the loss of my mum. There are a few things I have found not only helpful, but essential in my ability to hold space for others while dealing with bereavement myself.

Making full use of supervision is a must, allowing me to show up as the best version of myself as a counsellor and coach for my clients, while also maintaining professional and ethical practice.

Getting my own therapy also helped a lot, and I cannot recommend it enough. Having a safe space to share your feelings is an important step towards acceptance and healing.

This, along with practising self-care, supported me in putting my own personal boundaries in place. Only after I was truly beginning to take care of myself was I able to return to confidently and purposefully helping my clients. These boundaries included not returning to work before I felt genuinely ready to, and when I did return, choosing to work on a part-time basis to assess how I would be and how much I could manage. I eased myself back into the "helper" role, as it were.

It also meant not working with bereaved clients for a while after my return. My workplace was incredibly supportive, and it was actually their suggestion to do this. They redirected any bereaved clients to another counsellor, which was extremely helpful during this time, as this work may have been triggering for me and could have affected my ability to help those clients in the way they needed. This is also an important part of being a therapist: being open and honest about your ability and capacity to work with certain clients. I feel it would have been unethical of me to attempt to work with bereaved clients during that period.

It also included taking a step back from my coaching business for a few months to allow myself time to heal. I said no to any extra workload opportunities, acknowledging my need for 'me time' to relax and switch off. It involved recognising the signs when I was close to reaching capacity for all I could manage at that time and not overloading myself, thus avoiding the comeback of burnout I had previously experienced.

This was difficult for me in the beginning, as I am naturally a people pleaser in many aspects of my life. Normally, if someone asks me to do something for them, I will say 'Yes' straight away, but during this time, it became important for me to step back and say 'No' sometimes. And guess what? The world didn't end.

This was a new discovery for me - that I don't have to constantly be pleasing other people. Sometimes saying 'No' and having those boundaries is essential for our own well-being, healing, and strengthening our sense of self.

I also did some inner work. Digging deeper into myself to gain personal clarity and insight into my own feelings, and asking myself

"How am I showing up for my clients?"

"How am I showing up for myself?"

"Am I showing up with clarity and capacity to truly hold space for clients in their moment of need?"

If the answer was no, then I knew it was time to work on myself. Healing for not only my own benefit, but for the benefit of my clients.

Many people in a helping profession, such as therapists, social workers, family support workers, care assistants, psychologists, etc, are often drawn to this work, not accidentally, but because they have experiences of their own where they themselves have required support and help. This, in turn, often leads people to want to help and support others. These experiences can be powerful tools, but only when used with care and self-awareness. It is important that we allow our experiences to inform our empathy without allowing it to overshadow the client or direct their story.

Take self-disclosure, for example. In counselling, it is only deemed appropriate to mention your own experience when it is clearly in the client's best interest. If I ever mentioned my experience with grief in a session with a client, it would be brief and purposeful. I would never go into detail about my own bereavement and emotional encounter with grief when the session is about the client and their experience.

Although for some, that could be viewed as beneficial. To know that their therapist has an understanding of what they are going through. Or that they have had a similar experience and a level of knowledge on the subject that other therapists may not have. That feeling of being understood in a vulnerable moment could be viewed as valuable, depending on the client and the therapeutic relationship.

Also, just to know that during a time that feels so lonely and isolating, you are not alone in your grief. So, it really depends on the individual relationship between the counsellor and client, whether it would be deemed appropriate to self-disclose.

An important skill I have learned during my journey as a counsellor is the skill of just being with. Not fixing.

When I first set out to study counselling, I was under the impression that I would be able to 'fix' everyone's problems and make them feel better. That sentence alone sounds exhausting. Imagine carrying the weight of that. *FIXING* everyone.

I'm a human being. It was naïve of me to think it was within my power to *fix* anyone.

Maybe I wanted to heal others due to my own emotional experiences and early childhood loss. But the word 'fix' is a misconception that also perhaps some clients have about attending counselling.

"My counsellor will fix me."

"After I go to therapy, I will be fixed."

Instead, I discovered what I can do, and that is help people. I can support clients. I can sit with them in their pain. I can offer tools and techniques to help manage their challenges, but no counsellor, therapist, or coach can FIX anyone. And what does FIX someone mean? Stop the world from hurting them? Make it so that they never feel pain again? That is not possible, and after all, feeling and experiencing emotion is what makes us human.

We experience a full range of emotions throughout our lives, and it is ok to do so. It is ok to experience the difficult emotions. The pain, grief, sadness, nervousness and anger. The best thing we can do is acknowledge our emotions, recognise them, name them, and allow them to exist. Yes, it's uncomfortable, but the more we push those emotions away and pretend they don't exist, the harder they come back at us. Ignoring emotions doesn't make them disappear; it just buries them temporarily. Buried emotions have a way of showing up later. Through anxiety, destructive behaviours, or physical illness.

We need to feel to heal.

This means that in order to truly heal, we need to allow ourselves to feel what's going on inside. This might mean allowing ourselves to cry, talk, or simply admit that we are hurting.

It's not about staying stuck in those feelings forever. It is about acknowledging them, processing them, and letting them pass through us. It isn't some beautiful, transformative experience. Going through it is messy. It's crying in bed, it's taking your anger out on those you love, it's chaotic and painful, it's slow, and it changes you.

Think of grief like a deep wound or cut on your arm. You might ignore it and hope it goes away on its own, or you may cover it with a bandage or plaster and pretend it doesn't hurt. It might look ok for a while, but underneath that bandage we've stuck on there, there could be an infection because we didn't clean it before we taped it up. It might throb, swell, or cause more pain further down the line because you didn't take care of it properly. But if you stop, clean the wound and take care of it, and let it breathe, even though it stings at first, it gives your body a chance to heal.

Emotions work the same way. When we experience a loss, and we ignore the hurt or push down our feelings or pretend we are fine, the pain doesn't go away. It just sits inside, covered up, and can cause more problems later. Feeling our emotions is like cleaning the wound. It might hurt to face them at first, to cry, to talk, to feel. But that's what helps us heal properly from the inside out.

The Healing Power of Listening

Listening is the key to connection, understanding, healing, and transformation.

Active listening, another essential skill of a coach or counsellor, involves listening with intent. Recognising the meaning behind someone's words.

Does their body language, facial expressions, or tone align with their verbal communication?

When these subtleties are noticed and gently explored by someone, it fosters a sense of safety and security. In this space, people can be their authentic selves and begin to let go of what they are holding onto.

We often think that healing requires the perfect words. But sometimes, the most healing thing we can offer is our presence.

I'm going to use an example of my best friend, Kirsty. I had been texting her a few months ago when I was feeling down and sad, and she responded as she always does with love, listening, and empathy. We planned to meet up and go for a walk later in the week when we both had some free time. When that day came around, I didn't feel up to it. I texted her to cancel and ask if we could rearrange.

She said, "Of course".

Then a few hours later, my doorbell rang, and there she was standing at my front door with some iced coffees and brownies. We always joke that 'We are one' and that we always know what the other one is thinking. It makes sense since we have known each other our whole lives. Sometimes, I think she knows me better than I know myself.

What happened that day is that she heard that I didn't feel up for going for a walk, but she also heard behind those words that I still needed something or someone. So, she was there. Without me asking her to be. Her presence was enough. I didn't say an awful lot that day, but we sat there in my living room, drinking our iced coffees, and then after a while we did end up going for a walk, and I felt so much better for it. Just for seeing her, for being in the company of someone who truly gets it and sees me and knows what I need even if I don't.

Everyone needs a Kirsty in their life!

I am so grateful for her, not only through navigating the passing of my mum, or earlier in life, my dad, but throughout life in general.

Real connection begins with feeling heard and listened to, not being advised. Holding space for my clients builds trust, which is essential in a therapeutic relationship for transformation to be able to take place.

How can we heal if we don't feel heard? If we don't feel seen or understood, it makes us feel that we don't matter or that our feelings and experiences are insignificant. Listening validates someone's experience. And not just emotionally. Our nervous system begins to calm and heal in the presence of deep listening and understanding.

I talk about the nervous system a lot with clients, as I think it is important that we understand what our nervous system is and the vital role it plays. This is where things get a little bit into Neuroscience, but I am a geek when it comes to this. I love it. So, I'll try my best to share with you what this is, its importance and how it impacts us.

Understanding the Nervous System

The **central nervous system (CNS)** includes the brain and spinal cord. It is our 'control centre' of our body. It processes information and sends out instructions to the rest of the body.

The **autonomic nervous system (ANS)** runs automatically, regulating essential functions such as breathing, heart rate, digestion, and how we respond to stress or safety without us having to think about it. It has three main branches:

1. **Sympathetic Nervous System (SNS)** – Known as the *fight or flight* response. This is activated when we sense a threat, and it prepares our body to react quickly, like our ancestors would fight or run away, for survival. It speeds up the heart rate, tenses muscles, and sharpens focus. When someone talks about feeling anxious, their SNS is often activated. This is the brain/body's way of saying, "Something isn't right."

2. **Parasympathetic Nervous System (PNS)** – This is the *rest and relax* mode. It slows things down so we can recover, digest, and heal. This state feels like safety, calm, connection, and restoration.

3. **Dorsal Vagal Response (Freeze)** – When a situation feels too overwhelming, this branch may trigger a shutdown response. You might feel numb, exhausted,

spaced out, dissociated, or disconnected from yourself or your surroundings.

Our nervous system shapes how we feel, connect, and react, often without us consciously realising it. Trauma, stress, and grief can dysregulate our nervous system, making it difficult to feel safe, calm, or present. But with support and consistent practice, we can learn to regulate our nervous system again, which helps us feel more grounded, resilient, and connected to both ourselves and others.

This is something I work on with clients regularly: helping them understand and regulate their nervous system using calming techniques.

A Real-Life Example: The Job Interview

Imagine there's a situation that makes you feel nervous, like a job interview.

You don't know who you'll meet, what they'll ask, or if you will make a good impression. You feel under pressure to perform well. The stakes feel high. This can be perceived as a *threat*, and your body starts to react as you sit waiting to be called into that interview room.

Your breathing speeds up, your heart races. Your body temperature rises, and your blood pressure increases. You might get a headache, feel nauseous, dizzy, or faint. Or you might freeze, your mind goes blank when the interviewer asks you a question, even though you know the answer. You can't take in the questions, let alone respond. The experience might knock your confidence and make you hesitate before applying for other jobs.

When you get home, someone asks, "How did your interview go?" and you respond, "Terrible." They reply with "You must not have prepared enough!" You don't feel heard or supported, only judged. And that makes everything feel worse. You then associate this experience and the feelings it created with the next interview you go on, and so the cycle continues.

We label ourselves as 'being bad at job interviews', denting our confidence and making it difficult to get out of that negative thinking trap. Our thoughts affect our feelings, which affect our behaviours.

OR...

You are waiting to be called in for your interview and begin to notice your body's signals and name the feeling:

"Whoa, my heart rate is speeding up, and I feel hot. I must really care about this interview. I feel nervous, but I'm going to take off my jacket to cool down. Then I'll do some deep breathing, as my coach showed me. This will slow my heart rate and tell my brain that I'm calm, safe and in control."

Now you walk into the interview feeling more grounded. You can think clearly and are able to answer questions more confidently. Even if you don't get the job, you leave feeling proud, you pushed through discomfort and did it anyway. Later, when someone asks about the interview, and you tell them about your experience, they respond with:

"Sounds like you had quite the day. I'm sorry you felt nervous, but it seems like you handled it really well. Why don't you take the rest of the night to do something relaxing to help you reset for tomorrow?"

This version ends differently.

You feel more confident. You regulated your nervous system. You practised self-care. You felt *heard, seen, and supported.* And all of these things add up. Self-awareness, coping techniques, and compassion from others help regulate your nervous system and promote long-term healing and resilience.

Listening, true and intentional listening, is one of the most powerful gifts we can offer to others. When we are truly heard, it tells our brain, **"You're safe now".**

It validates our emotions as real and worthy of attention. It reduces feelings of isolation. Listening with empathy rather than with solutions allows people to feel safe, seen, and valued. And when we feel safe, our nervous system responds. We begin to relax, to breathe more deeply and to settle. Healing doesn't always happen in the big, noteworthy moments; it often begins in the quiet presence of someone who truly listens.

Also, listening doesn't need to come from an outside source. It is just as important to listen to ourselves. Healing also comes from listening inward. Listening to our own grief, needs, body and intuition. Sometimes we need to turn down the volume of the outside world to hear what our inner voice is saying.

An example of this is last year, when I reached burnout. My body and mind were crying out for me to step back and rest and not dive into everything all at once, too soon. It took the help of a counsellor for me to realise that I had to look inward and listen to what my body was trying to tell me.

What I saw when I looked inwards was that I was dissociating. Dissociation (dorsal vagal response activation) is the mind's way of protecting us when things feel too overwhelming. It feels like being disconnected from your body, your emotions, or even from reality itself.

People often experience dissociation in different ways, but for some, it is like watching their life from a distance rather than truly living it. For others, it's a sense of numbness or fog, a way to "check out" when pain feels too intense to process all at once. And this is what happened to me.

This is our brain's attempt to create a sense of safety and protect us during or after unbearable emotional pain or distress. It is our nervous system telling us we have experienced something "too much, too fast, too soon", and in response, creates distance between you and the pain. See how clever our brains are?

This was me for basically one full year after Mum's death. The whole year of 2025, although there were some big monumental life experiences (buying a house, gaining my supervision qualification), is a bit of a blur to me.

While dissociation can be a coping mechanism, especially after trauma or loss, it can also leave us feeling isolated, confused, or detached from ourselves, others and life.

Wondering "Why haven't I cried yet?" or "This doesn't feel real."

Over time, as safety and support increase, our brains will usually begin to allow more access to these emotions. That protective wall will soften, and we can start to move towards our journey of healing. This often involves gently reconnecting with those parts of us that had to go 'offline' or 'shut down' to survive.

I invite you to pause in this moment, as you read this. What is your body telling you now? Are you holding tension in your muscles? Is your jaw clenched? Is your mind racing? Are you thinking about a 'to-do list' and a bunch of tasks that need completing?

Listen to your inner voice and what it is saying to you, and honour that however you can.

This is a small act of mindfulness, and mindfulness is a great way to relax, connect and be present and respect your own needs, both physical and mental.

As counsellors, coaches, or simply as human beings, we don't need to have all the answers. We don't need to fix anyone or offer them advice. What we *can* do is show up. Fully, compassionately, and without judgment. Without interrupting. Without mentally preparing our replies. When we hold space in this way, we invite healing. We invite transformation. We invite connection.

Because in the end, listening isn't just something we *do*, it's something we *offer*. And when that is done with presence and care, it can be the bridge between hurt and healing.

Finding Meaning in the Mess

As previously stated, I knew I wanted to go into a helping profession from when I was a teenager. I have always been told that I am naturally personable, easy to talk to, and people warm to me easily. I have always been a good listener and an empathetic person.

When I was 14 or 15 years old, I got a Saturday job in a hairdresser's in my village. When I turned 16, I left school and worked for them full-time. I did well in all my exams, and I feel people were shocked when I wanted to leave school so early at such a young age. I think my family thought I would continue studying because I found school quite easy without having to try too hard. This isn't me bragging by any means! Some people find school and studying difficult, but for me, it came quite naturally.

I worked in a few different hairdressers, gaining my qualifications and then decided it's not what I want to do with my life. It was around this time that I had the conversation with my gran that led to my lightbulb moment about becoming a counsellor, but I was unsure where to start. I didn't really look too much into studying counselling at this time, but the seed was planted.

After that, I had various jobs in the hospitality industry. Working in bars, hotels, restaurants, etc. Until I decided to move to Tenerife. Then, when I returned to Scotland after Uncle Barry's passing, I knew it was time to start my career, and that's when I returned to college and University and got my honours degree.

While studying, I managed to get a few placements to gain some practical experience of working with people in an emotion-focused setting, including Macmillan Cancer Support. During this time, people would often say to me;

"That must be so difficult after what you went through with your dad"

But actually, I really enjoyed working in this capacity. It was a lovely, welcoming space with a warm and friendly environment, and I loved that people had a place to come to if they were struggling with their own cancer diagnosis or that of someone they loved. Still, it became clear to me that my true calling was to work with children and young people.

During my time at University, I secured a placement with a counselling organisation based in schools - and I loved it! I was fortunate enough to get a few different placements with them in primary schools that I could do while studying and working at the same time.

Shortly after graduating, I managed to get a job with an organisation, counselling children and young people in high schools. I was nervous about transitioning from primary to high school students. Primary counselling is very play-oriented. Children express themselves through art and play (just like I did, drawing that "faraway house" when I was nine). But I adapted quickly to my new role and found it incredibly fulfilling. I love my job working in CYP counselling, and my schools are fantastic. I have been there for 4 years, and it is the best decision I have ever made.

At the time when I was at university, I reconnected with Ian, my first boyfriend and first love from when we were teenagers. We got back together, and within six months, my pup Dennis and I had moved in with him.

Ian was really into hillwalking and climbing Munros, and I got into it too. To date, I've climbed 73 Munros (Scottish mountains over 3,000 feet). Together, Ian and I have completed the West Highland Way and climbed Ben Nevis, Mount Snowdon, and Scafell Pike (the highest mountains in Scotland, Wales, and England), along with many other outdoor hiking adventures.

Our favourite spot is Glencoe. It holds so many memories for us. And this is where Ian chose to propose in 2021.

We had planned a Scottish road trip, our own version of the North Coast 500 (a scenic driving route around the Northern Highlands in Scotland), with a mixture of camping and hotels. The trip would, of course, include ticking a few Munros off the list as we went. Towards the end of the trip, we met up with my Uncle John (my dad's brother) and Auntie Viv for dinner while we were in Aviemore.

The next day, we made our way to the *Kingshouse Hotel* in Glencoe. A place we had passed many times but had never stayed in, always commenting on how beautiful it looked. So, we ended our trip in style and luxury, with an overnight there. A welcome change from the past few nights in a tent in cold and snowy

Aviemore in October. Aviemore was a fantastic experience, and we had a great time, but I was glad of a proper bed and some warmth and luxury by the time we reached Glencoe!

When we arrived at our room at The Kingshouse, I was greeted with a bunch of flowers, a box of chocolates, and a bottle of prosecco. What a lovely surprise! We had a few glasses of fizz, and then, while I was getting showered and ready for our dinner reservation, Ian popped out to "get a bag from the car", but really, he was retrieving the engagement ring he had hidden and carried with him the entire trip. Unbeknownst to me.

This was the moment when he also had a standoff with a wild Stag that was guarding the car. Every time Ian turned around, the deer rammed him with its horns. The things we do for love! He still has a video of the incident, and it makes me laugh to this day, every time I see it. Although he was lucky he wasn't injured.

Glencoe is a popular spot for sighting wild deer, and we have been lucky enough to spot them many times on our travels, but this incident was a bit too close!

During dinner, Ian popped the question with a stunning backdrop of Glencoe's natural beauty. It was so perfect. I was so surprised. He said he had already asked permission from my mum, my sister, my brother, and my uncle John (the night before, when we met them for dinner, sneakily without me seeing). As it was my dad's brother, he thought it would be fitting to ask his permission also. So, everyone knew except for me! I had been waiting for this day my whole life. I was so happy.

After the excitement had settled, we had our dinner, had a few more bottles of prosecco to celebrate, and then Ian went to bed. I think it had been a long day for him, building up the courage to propose on top of driving 85 miles that day. I spent the rest of the night video calling my friends and family to share the news.

The next morning, we were on cloud 9, leaving Glencoe to head back home.

It was straight into full wedding planning mode! The colour schemes, the bridal party, the dress, the cake, the venue, the flowers. I had albums upon albums in my phone of different ideas and designs! I love planning and organising, so this was so exciting for me.

I actually started to plan this wedding, mine and Ian's, when we were 14! As Ian likes to tell the story and embarrass me, I might as well add it in here.

I had a "Wedding Folder", planning out my future wedding. I nearly collapsed with embarrassment one day when I walked into my room and discovered Ian had found it and was reading through all my plans!

In the midst of all the planning and excitement, reality set in. **Who was going to walk me down the aisle?**

As my friends all started to get married, throughout our 20s, this was a big trigger for me. Watching their dads giving them away as they walked them down the aisle was always heartbreaking. It resurfaced a lot of emotion. Emotion I had hidden away for years. And this takes us back to the ***Grief Cycle*** from earlier. Here I was now in my 20s, thinking I had reached acceptance over my dad's death, only to find myself back at depression/bargaining.

Regarding my own wedding, there was no doubt in my mind that I had to ask my baby brother. At this stage, he was 27, so not so much a baby. That year at Christmas, I handed him his Christmas card with a scratch card inside, which, when he removed the top layer, read underneath;

"You have been the man of the house since you were 4 years old. Would you do me the honour of giving me away on my wedding day?"

He said he would be proud to do it.

On my wedding day, the fact that there were so many family members missing was really difficult, but I handled it way better than I thought I would. I was just excited to be getting married at all, as we had one heck of a scare a few days before!

The week before the wedding, Ian and I decided to have an 'Early Moon', a little getaway before the big day as our honeymoon wouldn't be happening for another few months. We thought we would enjoy a few days away in our favourite areas of Scotland, to de-stress and relax once all the organising and final preparations were completed.

It was truly fantastic. We headed up to the Isle of Skye for a few days, then to our favourite place, Glencoe, staying at the Kingshouse, where we got engaged. It really felt like a full-circle moment. From getting engaged here to sitting in the same spot, counting down the days until we get to say, "I do".

When arriving at Glencoe, we decided to do a hike called 'The Pap of Glencoe'. I loved this idea because it had 'PAP' in its name. My beloved grandpa. I felt like this would be a nice tribute to him before the wedding.

On the descent, Ian noticed he had a pain in his abdomen. That night, I woke up around 2 am to hear him pacing around our hotel room, on the phone to NHS 24, describing the pain he was in. He lay awake for hours afterwards, and as soon as it hit 7 am, he drove to the nearest pharmacy, as instructed to do by the call handler, and picked up some painkillers. After an hour or so, he said this had 'taken the edge off'.

That day, we had booked a champagne afternoon tea, looking out to the stunning scenery of mountains, hills, rivers and waterfalls. Ian said he was feeling better, so we decided to stay and finish off our holiday.

That day was so perfect. It was cold but dry and sunny. Unusual not to see rain in October in Scotland, so we felt like we had won the jackpot, weather-wise. The scenery, the food, the peace and tranquillity. I wish I could bottle that feeling. And once again, a stag appeared. Just like the night Ian proposed. It was just amazing.

I managed to get some beautiful photos of the stag in front of the mountain, Buchaille Etive Mor (probably the most photographed mountain in Scotland). You might recognise it from photos you may have seen. With the little white house sitting at the foot of the mountain. We have actually climbed that mountain too! It couldn't have been more picturesque, and I felt truly grateful, relaxed and ready for our wedding in a few days.

But then...

The next day, as we packed to go home, Ian said he was still in pain. As soon as we were home, he went to the doctor and was sent immediately to the hospital.

His *appendix had burst*. We couldn't believe it. The pain he must have been in. This was now Wednesday morning, and we were getting married on Saturday.

Panic set in.

The doctors scheduled him for emergency surgery that night. Everything was a rush. We couldn't believe this was happening.

Will Ian be ok? Do I cancel the wedding?

A million thoughts were running through my mind, and I had no clue where to start.

One of my best friends and bridesmaids, Laura, came and sat with me at home that night while Ian was in surgery. Another example of how showing up can be so important. Laura asked if I wanted company, and I said I would be ok on my own. It was late at night, and she had two young babies at home. I didn't want to put her out. Her next message was that she was coming over and bringing some chocolate with her too! My favourite thing. I'm extremely lucky to have the amazing friends that I do.

As we sat waiting on that phone call, it seemed like days before we heard any news.

Then, eventually, the call came.

"He is out of surgery, and it was a success. He will need to stay in the hospital for a few days, but *SHOULD* make the wedding."

Great news! He was ok, and that was the main thing. At this stage, I messaged all our guests to let them know what had happened and that, at the moment, everything was still going ahead as planned. They discharged Ian on Friday morning, and we headed straight to Stirling to our wedding venue. We literally just made it!

Ian used my dad's wading stick (from his fishing days) to help him walk down the aisle, which I thought was a lovely sentimental touch. He has since hung it on our living room wall in our new home as part of our Highland-themed décor. So, a part of my dad did manage to walk down that aisle after all.

Not only that, but Christopher did something incredibly thoughtful on our wedding day, too. He carried a photo of my dad in his jacket pocket as he walked me down the aisle - so that in a way, Dad was there giving me away too. I had no idea at the time. It wasn't until a few months later at Christmas that Christopher gave me the photo he carried of my dad, now beautifully framed, and told me what he had done on the wedding day. To say I was emotional would be an understatement. It was the most touching surprise and lovely gift.

By the time the morning of the wedding came, I was just so relieved everything was going ahead and that my husband was ok, that nothing else mattered. I didn't have time to overthink the small details; I was simply grateful.

Yes, things went wrong on the day, like every wedding day. My venue decorator forgot to bring the sashes to make bows around the wedding guest chairs, and she was distraught! She came to me the morning of the wedding so upset and so apologetic. I felt terrible for her! But in that moment, I was just so happy the day was going ahead, and everyone was ok, that chair bows were the last thing on my mind.

As previously mentioned, my mum had an awful accident earlier that year, breaking 3 vertebrae in her spine after a fall and being bed-bound for months with a neck brace drilled into her skull so that she couldn't move her head/neck. It was a terrible time for her. She couldn't make it to my hen do and just managed to get the neck brace off before my wedding. At the wedding, she still struggled with movement, but she was there, and that's all that matters.

Because little did I know that in 10 months time, she wouldn't be here.

It's really unbelievable to think about. I'm just so glad she made it for my big day because, honestly, I don't know what I would have done without her there. There were already so many people missing, I don't think I could have gone through with it without my mum there. The three of us, my sister, brother and I, were very close to our Mum. It had just been the four of us for so many years growing up.

On the morning of the wedding, I gave my mum a necklace. It was a chain with 2 silver hoops intertwined with each other, and it read *mother and daughter tied together forever.* She loved it, and there is a gorgeous photo of me giving it to her on that day and then us hugging. She never took it off from that day until her last. I now wear this necklace. I put it on me the day she passed away and will never take it off. It is a special memory for us and something I will cherish forever. Although it has a different meaning now.

We got our wedding video about a year after the wedding (a few weeks after mum had passed). I have watched it countless times, and the first 5/6 times I was crying my eyes out. Seeing her there - smiling, emotional, *present* - was both beautiful and heartbreaking. How could she not be here now?

The memories of the day are so emotional for me. In both Ian and Christopher's speeches, they honoured my mum, thanking her and acknowledging what an incredible job she did raising three kids under 10 on her own. You can see her holding back tears in the video. It was unusual for Mum to cry, so this must have been an extremely emotional day for her.

They are such precious memories, ones that still bring tears. But also, memories that are full of love.

I think throughout all of this, we have learned it's clear that life doesn't follow a script. It's unpredictable, messy, beautiful, and sometimes painful. But within that mess, we often find moments that define us. Moments that show us who we are and what truly matters.

For me, it wasn't just about planning a wedding, climbing mountains, or navigating last-minute emergencies. It's about being present. About recognising how far I'd come. From a teenager with a Saturday job in a hairdresser's planning her own future wedding, to becoming a counsellor and supporting others, all while navigating a healing journey herself. It was about honouring my past, celebrating the milestones, embracing the joy of the present, and holding close the people who shaped me, especially those no longer here.

There is meaning in the mess. There is strength in the struggle, although it often doesn't feel like it at the time. And sometimes, in the middle of chaos, we discover grace: in the form of a beautiful stag by a mountain, a meaningful silver necklace passed between hands, or a partner who shows up through his own pain when it matters the most.

I've learned that we don't always get the version of life we planned; mine has been far from it. My wedding folder from when I was a teenager certainly didn't account for all the mishaps that were to come and the family members that would be missing from my special day. But sometimes, if we're open to it, we find something meaningful in amongst the mess. And in that, there is healing.

Surviving the Storm

Grief can feel like being caught up in a storm you never saw coming. One minute, life is as it was, and then the next, everything changes. The skies darken. The ground beneath you shifts. You feel lost with no map or satnav to get you back to where you were.

In the middle of this chaos, looking after yourself might feel impossible. And yet, it is during this time of unexpected upheaval that you need care the most.

This chapter focuses on gently guiding ourselves towards self-care in bereavement. Not the polished kind you might see on social media, the kind that makes you wonder if you are doing it wrong - but the real, raw, moment by moment, tending to your mind, body and spirit when needed.

Start with the basics -

Grief can strip life down to 'survival mode', so in that moment, make sure you are surviving.

Drink water – Staying hydrated is essential, especially when you're going through emotional stress or grief. You might not feel thirsty, or even notice how little you've had to drink, but your body still needs water to function properly. Dehydration can intensify fatigue, headaches, and brain fog, all of which can already feel heightened when you're grieving.

Try to keep a glass or bottle of water nearby and take small sips throughout the day, even if it's just a little at a time.

Eat when you can - Grief can disrupt your appetite and make the idea of eating feel overwhelming. If full meals feel like too much, that's okay. Aim for small, manageable portions throughout the day. Something as simple as a piece of fruit, a handful of nuts, some toast, or a smoothie can make a difference. Try to include a few things that offer vitamins, protein, or fibre, even in tiny amounts. These small acts of nourishment support your body and, in turn, your emotional resilience.

You're not just feeding your body; you're gently helping it begin the process of healing and recovery.

Rest (even when you can't sleep) – I remember lying awake for hours and hours, the days, weeks and months after mum passed away. My husband and I would still go to bed at our normal time, and even after he had drifted off, I would just lie there. Even though I was exhausted, I couldn't sleep. My mind was doing somersaults. But as long as you rest and try to relax your body. Just lying with your eyes closed, more often than not, you will eventually drift off to sleep. And if not, at least you are resting your body. It is important during this time that you don't beat yourself up for not sleeping. Telling ourselves "I SHOULD" be doing this or "I NEED" to do this is shame-inducing. It makes us feel worse and more tense, which will make sleeping feel even more difficult.

Try to do something relaxing to help you drift off to sleep.

Meditation – If it is still really difficult to sleep, try listening to relaxing sounds (relaxing music, guided meditation or nature sounds). Listening to nature sounds has been scientifically proven to help us relax, as our brains are wired to listen out for safety. For example, birds chirping. That noise back in our ancestors' day would signify that there were no predators around, so we could fully relax without fear, and this still has the same effect on us to this day. My personal favourite relaxing nature sounds are raindrops and waves (water baby!)

Meditation helps clear our mind, and listening to the sounds of nature has a calming effect on the body and brain, which can help lower our stress levels, slow our heart rate and breathing, regulate our emotions, and support better sleep.

Move gently - When you are grieving or under emotional strain, even the idea of moving your body can feel like too much. That's why the focus here is on *gentle* movement, not exercise for fitness or goals (unless you want to, of course), but movement for release, grounding and care. This could be as simple as walking around the block, stretching in your living room, doing a few minutes of yoga, or just taking some slow, deep breaths while standing by a window.

Movement, no matter how small, can help emotions shift and circulate. Grief often settles in the body as tension in the shoulders, tightness in the chest or a heaviness that's hard to name. Gentle movement helps to loosen those stuck places. It reconnects you with your body in a kind, non-demanding way. There's no pressure here, just an invitation to move through some of the weight, little by little, on your own terms.

Make space for your feelings - You don't have to "be strong". You don't have to "hold it together". Let yourself cry, scream, or sit in silence. Grief has no rulebook. It is not tidy; it is not linear. Some days it might bring sadness – you might cry without warning, other days it might bring numbness where you feel nothing at all or even strange moments of peace or laughter or guilt for feeling peaceful or experiencing laughter. But all of this, all of it is normal.

Let the waves come.

You don't need to fight them or try to hold them back. You don't need to make sense of them; you just need to hold your head above the water, and the more we stop trying to fight our way through the waves, the easier we float. Permit your feelings to exist. They are part of your healing.

Journalling, voice notes, or therapeutic letter writing can create a safe space for grief to breathe when talking about it feels too much.

Journalling is something I usually recommend to clients who are on a healing journey. Journalling is an activity where we write down our thoughts and feelings, which allows us to start to make sense of them and begin to heal through accepting and processing our emotions.

It is a personal practice. There is no fear of judgment attached to expressing yourself because all your thoughts and feelings are private. You don't need to show anyone (unless you want to, which can also be a good way of making your feelings known to others without having to say them out loud). It helps us gain clarity and lower levels of stress. Regular writing can help boost our self-esteem and aid mindfulness by encouraging reflection and personal growth, as well as improving sleep and gently moving forward towards any goals we might have.

There are lots of different ways to approach journalling. For me, I would use a notebook and a pen because that's how my brain works and processes information. Writing has always been healing for me and something I enjoy. But I know for others, the thought of writing regularly is their worst nightmare.

If the thought of writing makes you wince, then there are different ways we can approach it. For example, journalling through creativity. Some people prefer to draw, colour or paint their emotions through art. Some people like to create characters or stories, and I have heard many clients say that they have found it useful to express their emotions through poetry. There are also journalling apps we can get for our phones, or if you prefer to type, create a journal on your notes function on your phone, iPad or laptop. It's about finding out what works for you.

And if writing at all is not possible, then use voice notes. Record yourself speaking out loud. Express yourself to yourself. Taking away again, that fear of judgment we sometimes have when speaking to others. Say how you feel and don't hold back. No one is going to hear your notes unless you show them, so let go. Take a deep breath and let it all out.

Therapeutic letter writing is another valuable technique I often use with clients in the counselling room, but you can also do this on your own. You are writing a letter to someone. They are never going to receive this letter or read the contents, but it is a therapeutic way for you to let go and say all the things you want to say to them. This could be a letter to a loved one who has passed away, a letter to someone who has wronged you and you still harbour feelings around that, or a letter to a past or future version of yourself. This can be really powerful and instrumental in our healing journey.

Find your anchors –

You need something consistent and steady to hold on to when everything feels rocky and uncertain. These are your anchors. Small practices that help you feel grounded and maintain your wellbeing.

They might be:

- A cup of tea or coffee in the same mug each morning
- A short walk at the same time each day
- A daily journal entry
- Watching a TV programme or listening to music that feels familiar, enjoyable and comfortable
- A regular morning or nighttime routine
- A structured check-in with yourself. "How am I feeling today?" Each morning when you wake up or each night before you go to sleep. This can be a good prompt to start a journal entry with, too.

When everything feels in turmoil, through the hectic chaos and unpredictability of grief, some sort of constant, no matter how small, is necessary. Identify what brings you a sense of calm and stability. Think of people, activities or objects. Pets can be a great source of consistency and comfort during this time. I know my pup Dennis was for me.

Look for what or who makes you feel comforted and supported during this difficult time. Check in with yourself regularly to see how and if your anchors are working and make adjustments when needed. If they are no longer serving you, then look to make a change. Experiment with different options. What works for someone else may not work for you, and vice versa.

Also, make your anchors a priority. Make an effort to incorporate them into your day. By doing this, you create a foundation of stability and resilience to help you navigate difficult times.

Grief reshapes us. It creates a new place where love and pain coexist. And in the midst of that reshaping, our needs become more tender and more immediate. We don't need perfection; we need presence, and we need kindness, especially from ourselves.

If you take anything away from this chapter, let it be this: caring for yourself in grief is not a luxury; it is a necessity. It doesn't need to look pretty or follow a timeline. It just needs to be honest. If today all you could do was drink an extra glass of water or sit in stillness for five minutes, that's enough. If you managed a short walk, or let the tears fall, or wrote a few words in a journal, you showed up for yourself, and that's all that matters.

This is not about "getting over" your grief. There is no finish line. A few weeks ago, I did not feel ok, and this week I do feel ok. And I'm sure that will change many times before the end of the year. And that is all ok!

This is about learning to live alongside your loss. With time, some care, and a bit of gentleness, you will find that the chaos becomes less frequent or less fierce.

You will find moments of peace between the storms, and hopefully, over time, those moments of peace become more regular. You may even begin to notice small, quiet joys again.

Take it one step at a time. One moment or even one breath. Healing doesn't mean forgetting; it means remembering with love.

You are not alone in this. And you are doing better than you think.

The Strength They Left Behind

My personal experience of grief has felt unusual for my age. I don't know many people in their early 30s who have experienced half the bereavement that Louise, Christopher, and I have endured. But within that reality, I want to take a moment to honour the strength I see in the three of us.

I've already mentioned the positive factors that may have helped us. Our support systems, friends, family, and counselling and honestly, just having each other. I have recently reflected on just how complex and individual grief truly is. And don't get me wrong, there have been days, weeks, months for each of us where we have felt completely overwhelmed and unable to cope. But that strength, that resilience, comes from somewhere. And for us, I believe it was a mixture of our support systems, being there for each other, and having our mum as a role model growing up.

Watching her as we grew, navigating her own grief, challenges, and changes. Being strong and staying strong for herself and her three kids. Having to go back to work while raising her 3 kids alone as a single mother. A hardship, I think we didn't truly appreciate until we were adults ourselves.

Although it might not feel like it now, you have that strength too. That strength and resilience that comes from being kind to yourself.

Be gentle and give yourself grace because it is needed. Ask yourself, what would you say to a friend who was grieving right now? What would you say to your inner child if they were grieving? Would you tell them that they should be over it by now? Would you tell them that they should be back to normal by now? Of course not. So please be mindful of the conversations you have with yourself.

Negative self-talk and shame can quickly spiral into a cycle that damages self-esteem and fuels feelings of worthlessness. Remember, the person you speak to most in your life is *yourself* - through your thoughts, your inner voice, and your self-perception. Please choose words that are kind, gentle, and compassionate. Speak to yourself the way you would speak to someone you love

It's about listening to your body and your mind and giving yourself what you need in that moment. If that's rest and recovery, then prioritising self-care is crucial. If it's time alone or perhaps more interaction with others, then honour that. Sometimes it means reconnecting with others. Sometimes it means reflecting and focusing inward.

For Christopher, that looked like joining the Navy, bravely giving his energy a purpose and focus on a new beginning. Louise also chose to do some travelling with friends. For me, it meant taking time off work to recover and stepping back from things for a while.

Whatever the path, what matters is recognising that there is **no one right way to grieve**. Everyone handles bereavement differently, and that's ok. The most important thing is that we give ourselves the grace and compassion to just be. To know it is a painful and horrible time, but it won't always be like this. **This too shall pass.**

There will come a time when things won't feel so heavy. When the weight lifts and things start to feel 'normal' again. Whatever 'normal' means after a loss. This is something that I have to remind myself of still regularly. Life continues. Not because we forget, but because we carry our grief forward with us. Life will feel different. And that's ok too.

The emotions that come with grief are wide and varied: sadness, shock, regret and guilt (some often complex, unsettling emotions that may arise during bereavement when we think about the 'What ifs' 'I should have done...' 'I should have said...'), love, anger, even relief - another complex emotion that may arise when we know our loved one is no longer in pain. These are all valid and all part of the process.

Despite my training as a counsellor, I won't pretend that knowing how grief works makes living through it any easier. I may understand the theory, but I'm still human. I still carry the same weight everyone else does when someone they love is gone. My training has helped me to support others through their grief, but it hasn't made my own any less painful.

That said, my grief has shaped my life, my career, and my worldview. It has shaped my experiences and my choices. It has influenced how I show up for others and for myself. It has deepened my empathy and taught me the importance of patience, especially with myself. But this is something that has taken a long time for me to acknowledge (and that's with the added benefit of my counselling training). My journey with bereavement started 25 years ago, and I'm still trying to navigate that loss.

One thing I believe passionately is that society does not always support grief well enough. We need more compassion, more understanding, and more space for healing. Especially when it comes to something as significant as parental or child loss. Expecting someone to "bounce back" to normal life after such a life-altering experience is not only unfair, it can be highly damaging. Forcing people back to work too soon creates a ripple effect: burnout, anxiety, disconnection, emotional overwhelm, and ultimately, poor mental health.

So how do we avoid that spiral?

We begin by checking in with ourselves - genuinely and often. Then we reach out.

That might mean speaking to a counsellor or therapist, someone you connect with and feel safe with. Because the truth is, not every therapist is the right fit for every person, and that's completely okay. The connection in the therapeutic relationship is everything. It takes time, trust, and a willingness to show up from both sides. Without that connection, real healing is difficult. But with it, change becomes possible, and transformation begins.

I know this from personal experience from both sides of the therapy room. As a child, I wasn't ready to connect with my counsellor. I didn't have the words or the readiness. And now, as a therapist myself, I sometimes see that same hesitation in the younger clients. They're not always ready to engage, and that's okay, too. Readiness can't be forced - it comes in its own time. The important thing is that the door remains open so that when a child does feel ready to engage, they can.

Self-care also plays a vital role. Do something for yourself. It doesn't need to be a weekend at a spa (although that sounds lovely!) It can be something as simple as going to bed earlier, taking vitamins, eating healthier, drinking more water, reading a good book, looking up at the stars, watching a beautiful sunrise or sunset, journalling, colouring, drawing, painting, dancing, going for a walk, getting up 20 minutes earlier to have a coffee in peace before the rest of the household wakes up, buying yourself a bunch of flowers while doing the weekly shop. Something small from you to you.

Ask yourself: *How do I feel when I do this?* And keep checking in. Become aware of your nervous system - what triggers a response and how you regulate it to tackle dysregulated feelings. These moments of attention and care help us build self-awareness, our ability to notice how we feel, what we need, and what our bodies are trying to tell us. What signals is your body giving you? Do you need to slow down? Rest more? Be still?

I recently came across a quote that stayed with me:

"Meditate each day. Even if it's for 10 minutes. If you can't find the time to meditate for 10 minutes, you should meditate for an hour."

Because so often, when we feel we are too busy to care for ourselves, that's when we need it the most. You simply can't pour from an empty cup.

If you're finding it difficult to engage with self-care or build self-awareness, find someone who can help. It's what I do every day. I walk with people through their grief, anxiety, burnout, or confusion. Together, we explore the pain and the possibility of change.

You are not alone.

Grief has left its mark on my life in ways I never could have predicted. It has changed how I move through the world, how I connect with others, and how I care for myself. But within the pain, there has also been growth. A deeper understanding of myself. A stronger connection with the people I love. A renewed commitment to compassion - both for others and for myself.

The truth is that healing doesn't mean forgetting. It means learning how to carry what has been lost while still allowing yourself to live and to eventually feel joy again. It means recognising that even in the hardest seasons, there is hope. And sometimes, the most powerful thing we can do is simply allow ourselves to be exactly where we are without judgment, without rushing, and without expectation.

Healing takes time. Be kind to yourself.

The Gift in Grief

Who would believe that there is actually a positive somewhere in all this mess? A gift in grief.

I feel that my experience with grief has put me in a unique position to be able to support others. From both working with children and young people and my childhood experience of parental loss to losing close family members during early adulthood, as well as another unexpected and traumatic parental bereavement. I have come to understand grief from many angles.

I believe that counsellors bring different forms of empathy to their work, and those who have experienced personal loss or bereavement may sometimes have a particular understanding of the feelings that accompany deep grief. Although counsellors without this experience are still fully capable of offering skilled, compassionate, and effective support. Ultimately, it's about finding the counsellor who feels right for you, and for some people, a shared lived experience can help strengthen the therapeutic bond we discussed previously.

When working with bereaved clients, there are occasions when I may share a small part of my own experience, but only when it feels therapeutically appropriate and genuinely in the best interest of the client. As mentioned earlier, thoughtful and minimal self-disclosure can be a powerful tool when used with care and intention.

My aim in sharing is never to shift the focus onto myself, but to offer a sense of connection that may help the client feel less isolated in what they're going through.

I often reflect on how meaningful that kind of understanding might have been for me as a child. I didn't feel a strong connection with my counsellor as a child, and I wonder whether knowing they had lived through something similar might have helped me feel safer to open up and more able to benefit from the support that was offered.

When your family is grieving as well, it can naturally be harder for you to talk openly at home. This isn't due to any lack of care, but simply because everyone is navigating their own emotions, and some may worry about adding to the sadness around them, becoming overwhelmed themselves, or not knowing how to ask for support.

These feelings can be heavy and confusing for us to carry alone. In those moments, a brief, gentle and thoughtful expression of shared humanity can sometimes open a small window of connection. And sometimes, that's all it takes to offer someone a sense of hope and safety.

Grief can feel incredibly isolating, both for children and for adults. Especially when it seems like no one else your age has experienced it. I felt this deeply after losing a parent as a child, and I've felt it again as an adult.

It's very rare to meet someone my age who has lost *both* parents. That being said, my friend, Cat, is one of the few people who, unfortunately, has also experienced it. Her lovely mum, Margaret, passed away not long after my mum, and we had both already lost our dads. So, in an unfortunate and heartbreaking way, we found ourselves in a shared experience that not many others around us could relate to.

While it's devastating that we both know this kind of loss, it's also been comforting to have someone who does understand - to grieve alongside someone who *gets it* without needing everything explained. I think that mutual understanding and timing has been extremely powerful in helping us both get through it.

When it feels like everyone else has moved on after your loss, it's so helpful to know there is someone you can sit with and talk about it with and get upset with or vent your anger and stress to and laugh about things without judgment or fear because they know exactly how it feels. And sometimes, that mutual understanding is everything.

I believe that, of all the loss and bereavement I have experienced, some good must come of it. And I believe that is to support others in their grief or any other difficulties they may be experiencing. That is not to say my experience and feelings will be the same as someone else who is grieving, but understanding and empathy are sometimes enough for a client in that moment. Enough for them to feel heard and understood, which is a huge stepping stone to processing grief.

My second hope is that by writing this book, due to my own unfortunate experiences with grief, it will help someone else. If it helps even one person who is grieving, then it has served its purpose. I hope it offers some comfort, creates space for self-compassion, and perhaps offers tools which support the beginning of a healing journey.

More than anything, I hope you, the reader, have found something within these pages, whether it is a moment of self-care, a glimmer of hope that the weight you're carrying won't always feel so heavy, or simply the reassurance that you are not alone.

If you are struggling with grief, please don't hesitate to reach out to someone. There will always be someone to listen to you with acceptance and without judgment. You are never a burden.

I hear this phrase a lot during sessions with clients, **"I don't want to be a burden to anyone".** You are not. I'm sure people around you would rather know what you are feeling, to be able to try and support you, rather than having you carry it all on your own. If speaking to a family member feels too difficult, then speak to a friend, teacher, neighbour, doctor, therapist or coach. Whoever you feel comfortable with.

I'm currently operating a waiting list for one-to-one clients at the moment, but offering free consultation sessions, so if you would like to connect and explore some options to help process your grief, please do not hesitate to get in touch via the website or email, and we will support you in any way we can.

www.heatherhigginscoaching.com

heatherhigginscoaching@outlook.com

Thank you for choosing to read my book, 'Guided by Grief'. I hope that somewhere in these pages, you have found something that resonated with you.

If you are experiencing grief at the moment, please, if you take anything away from this book, just know that you are not alone. You are not a burden. There are always people willing to help you. And although it may feel like the end of the world, I promise you it's not.

Be kind to yourself. Be gentle. Give yourself the grace and compassion you deserve during this difficult time. Allow yourself to rest. There are no expectations here, only space to heal.

Afterword

Grief changes you, but it doesn't have to break you.

I started writing this book around 8 months after my mum had passed away, so I was right in the midst of grief. Which I feel is evident in these pages, as I edit and read them back. But I decided not to change anything as things changed for me. It felt important to honour that stage of grief and how I was feeling at the time - feelings that could very much resonate with someone else.

And that was the whole point of the book.

Still navigating my own journey, and as someone who has always enjoyed writing, I thought it would be a nice way to help me process my own thoughts and feelings. What started as a journalling exercise, however, turned into a published book. By combining my own personal grief diaries with my experience of working in mental health, I hope I can help others in some way navigate their own experiences with grief.

Days turned into months, which in the blink of an eye turned into a year. I was still writing this when my mum's 1st anniversary came up. I had to step away from writing for a while during that time. The lead-up to that week was horrendous. Everyone always says -

"The firsts are the hardest"

The first Christmas without them, your first birthday without them, their first birthday... the list goes on. And they are not wrong. I had in my mind that on that first anniversary, I would be re-living the trauma all over again.

This was the week we also laid her ashes at the cemetery, at the same place as her mum, dad, and brother. That was a very emotional moment for me.

I stood at that gravestone in disbelief; it was hard for me to process. The whole family, now here laid to rest.

I cried. Christopher and Louise both came over and hugged me. It felt so final for me somehow.

But later that day, that sunny Sunday in August, we decided to have an impromptu BBQ at our house. Lots of friends popped by throughout the day to see us, show their support and spend the day with us. They brought gifts, food, and drink, and we raised a glass to Karen and actually had a really nice day.

I realised I had been dreading that week so much that I had built it up in my head to be ten times worse than it actually was. Yes, it was emotional. Yes, it was sad and scary. But we got through it. As we always have.

And in the nicest way possible, it felt like now that's done, now the first anniversary is over, and her ashes are buried, I suddenly felt a bit lighter somehow. It is a complex and confusing time, but it felt to me, in some small way, that there is a ray of hope in moving forward.

Fast forward a few weeks, Ian, Louise, Christopher and I were discussing what our plans would be for Christmas day, and as we sat and spoke about our limited options, the three of us had the same thought, and we said -

"Wow, we really are orphans now!"

We have no one else to make plans with or buy gifts for or organise the day around. It was a hard realisation. I am aware that this is the second Christmas without mum, but the first year, I think we were still in so much shock and were just trying to get through the holidays as much as possible. We were still in survival mode, and honestly, when I think back to that first Christmas after Mum's passing, it is all a blur to me.

I have heard it said before that for some, the second year of grief is often tougher than the first. This is because for some, the first year can be so full of shock, dissociation or numbness, especially following a sudden or unexpected bereavement.

But after the first year, things around us begin to settle. Life starts to go "back to normal," and there can be a quiet expectation that we should have moved on or be "over it" by now.

People appear to forget what we are going through. Life goes on for them. And for some, this is when the grief hits hardest.

When the shock fades, we are left with the sadness and the realisation that life has changed forever - that things will never be the same.

If you are in your first year of grief, please don't take this to mean your second year will feel worse. Some people find the second year gentler, and this is when they can begin their healing journey. It looks different for everyone. No two people grieve in the same way, not even siblings who have experienced the same loss.

When this year's festive season came around, it was actually enjoyable. Yes, there was sadness. Yes, we missed our family. Yes, we had wobbly, emotional moments. But we decided to create new traditions this year, without ever forgetting the old ones.

Ian cooked dinner, and we hosted Christmas for the first time in our new home. It was a really good day, filled with friends, food, and laughter.

The New Year looked different, too. Last year, I remember feeling low, withdrawn, and numb yet overwhelmed. This year, Ian and I took a trip to a remote part of the Lake District and stayed in a cabin for a few nights, complete with a hot tub, nature walks, and pub lunches.

It was calm and unpressured - just perfect and just what was needed.

We brought in the new year with some prosecco in the hot tub while playing old Scottish tunes on our phones and looking at the stars, chatting and laughing. No party, no pressure, just us.

It turns out that the thought of the festive period was much worse than the actual time itself. Just the same as mums 1 year anniversary. Sometimes we build these things up so much that the thought becomes unbearable, but when you have support around you, you find you are stronger than you think you are.

If my journey has taught me anything, it's that there is light, even in the darkest moments. It doesn't always arrive dramatically. Often, it begins as a twinkle or a spark. In the form of a small gesture. A gentle word. An unexpected conversation.

An invitation. A memory that makes you smile through the tears. Or maybe it's the quiet presence of a friend who shows up at your door with coffee, no words needed, just the sense that someone sees you and knows you're hurting.

These are the moments that matter, the moments of hope that we will get through this.

These moments don't erase the pain, but they remind us that alongside the ache, there is still connection, love and life happening around us, and within us.

Another example of this is on my dad's birthday this year, on Jan 16th 2026, he would have been 65. This is also around the 25th anniversary of when he passed. I decided that this year, I wanted to go and visit his grave. This is something new for me. I had never had the want or urge to do this before. So, I went and bought flowers and drove myself to the cemetery where he is buried.

During this visit, I actually experienced a feeling of peace and comfort. This was surprising to me. At the age of (almost) 35, I didn't experience the anxiety, the nervousness, the nausea I previously had. I felt close to him. I spoke to him for the first time and felt a sense of not wanting to leave. Was this me reaching acceptance? 25 years later?

This just goes to show there is no timeline. And as discussed during the grief cycle, acceptance is a stage we can flow in and out of. Maybe I will flow out of it again, but for now, I'm happy that I experienced that feeling of peace and comfort. Which may sound strange, but it is an example of how complex the emotions are that surround our loss. Maybe I will visit more often now.

My hope in writing this book and sharing pieces of my own story is that you have felt a little less alone in yours. That you have found comfort in knowing your experience is valid, your feelings are allowed, and there is no one "right" way to grieve.

Grief isn't linear. It isn't neat or predictable. As you can probably tell from these pages, my experience has been anything but linear.

My narrative changes as the chapters progress, as things begin to feel different for me. This is my story, told as I experienced grief in real time. If Louise, Christopher, or anyone else had written this book, it would look very different.

Sometimes you have a good day, and it feels like progress. Other times, it feels as though you are starting all over again.

One moment, you may feel a sense of peace, and the next, a wave of sadness may crash over you without warning. This is not a sign of failure; it is a reflection of love, memory, and humanity.

Being sad after a bereavement is normal. It is the most normal thing in the world. So often, we beat ourselves up for being sad for "too long" or not following the 'timeline' people expect us to follow when grieving.

But there is no timeline. **It doesn't exist.**

Like when you are doing OK and then experience the sudden pain of picking up your phone to call or text your mum to innocently ask her a question about cooking, or to remind her that a TV programme you both like is starting tonight, or to settle an argument between my brother or sister and me or tell her about something funny that happened today, and then you realise.

It hits you again.

And again.

They are no longer here.

That constant reminder is a pain like no other.

But, with time, you begin to understand that these moments of reaching out are not signs of "going backwards" - they are signs of love. They are the confirmation of a relationship that shaped you, and that matters.

What I've learned is this: healing doesn't mean forgetting. It doesn't mean "moving on" or erasing the past.

It means learning to carry both love and loss at the same time. It means making space for the complexity of your emotions and allowing them to exist without judgment. It means finding your way forward, even if it's just one breath, one step, or one quiet moment at a time.

This is not easy work. But you are doing it.

Simply by showing up, by being willing to care for yourself, by reading this book, you are tending to yourself and your healing.

So, as we reach the end of this together, I want to leave you with this truth:

You are not alone.

You are not "too much."

You are not a burden.

You are not broken.

You are not taking too long.

You are not grieving too hard.

You are not moping.

You are human. You are grieving. You are doing the best you can, and that, my darling, is enough.

There will be days when your progress feels invisible. Days when the heaviness returns.

But in those days, you haven't lost anything. Healing is not a straight path. Every act of care you give yourself, no matter how small, is part of that journey.

Permit yourself to rest. To feel. To speak your truth. To reach out.

Give yourself time, compassion, and patience.

And if all you can do today is get through, sometimes, that's more than enough.

Thank you for allowing me to walk beside you in this part of your story. And thank you for joining me in mine. I hope, in some small way, this book has helped you feel seen, supported, and hopefully reminded you of your own strength.

References

Bowlby, J. (1969). *Attachment and loss: Vol. 1. Attachment.* New York: Basic Books.

Kübler-Ross, E. (1969). *On death and dying.* New York: MacMillan.